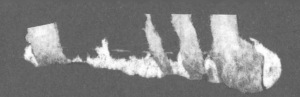

WITHDRAWN

GW00671041

THE LYLE'S GOLDEN SYRUP® COOKBOOK

THE
LYLE'S
GOLDEN SYRUP®
COOKBOOK

OVER 100 SWEET AND SAVOURY RECIPES, CELEBRATING
THE NATION'S FAVOURITE STICKY STAPLE

WITHDRAWN

First published in Great Britain by
Simon & Schuster UK Ltd, 2016
A CBS Company

Published under licence from Tate & Lyle Sugars.
Lyle's Golden Syrup is a registered trademark of
European Sugar Holdings S.a.r.l

Recipe, design and photography copyright © Simon & Schuster 2016

This book is copyright under the Berne Convention.
No reproduction without permission.
All rights reserved.

ISBN 978-1-4711-4888-0
ISBN 978-1-4711-5644-1 (Paperback)

10 9 8 7 6 5 4 3 2 1

Simon & Schuster UK Ltd
222 Gray's Inn Road, London WC1X 8HB
www.simonandschuster.co.uk
Simon & Schuster Australia, Sydney
Simon & Schuster India, New Delhi

A CIP catalogue record for this book
is available from the British Library

Printed and bound in China
Colour Reproduction by Aylesbury Studios Ltd, UK

Notes on the recipes
EGGS Use medium eggs, unless otherwise
stated. Pregnant women, the elderly and children
should avoid recipes with eggs which are not
fully cooked or raw.

FRUIT AND VEGETABLES Our recipes use
medium-sized fruit and vegetables, unless otherwise stated.

MICROWAVES If we have used a microwave
in any of our recipes, the timings will be for
an 850 watt microwave oven.

PREP AND COOKING TIMES These are approximate
and meant to be guidelines. Prep time includes all the
steps up to and following the main cooking time(s).
Cooking times may vary according to your oven.
Before serving chicken, always check that there is no
pink meat and that the juices run clear by piercing the
thickest part of the flesh with a sharp knife or skewer.

SPOON MEASUREMENTS These are level. 1 tablespoon = 15 ml,
1 teaspoon = 5 ml.

Image on pages 6-7: promotional poster dated c.1890

CONTENTS

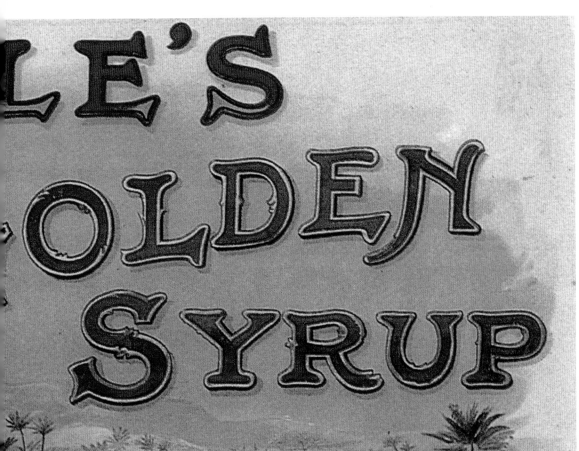

LE'S GOLDEN SYRUP

THE Best & Purest to be had

WARRANTED PURE & WHOLESOME
FREE FROM
GLUCOSE and all IMPURITIES

in 1℔. 2℔. 4℔ & 14℔. Tins.

ABRAM LYLE & SONS,
LIMITED.
Sugar Refiners. LONDON.

THE LYLE'S STORY

It is among the oldest and most iconic brands in the world – an enduring Victorian legacy which holds pride of place in millions of kitchen storecupboards. Yet Lyle's Golden Syrup might never have been spooned from its familiar green and gold tin had it not been for a twist of fate in 1865.

That year, a Scottish transatlantic shipping company owned by Abram Lyle (right in illustration below) and his partner John Kerr docked a cargo of West Indies sugar cane at Greenock on the south bank of Scotland's River Clyde. On discovering the importer couldn't pay the freight charges, they agreed to take his sugar in lieu of the debt. It proved a canny move.

Lyle's expansion into the sugar trade coincided with that of another ambitious company run by a former Liverpool grocer, Henry Tate (left in illustration opposite), who owned a refinery in the city's Love Lane quarter. Over the next three decades these two families would become fierce business competitors, protective of their recipes and production secrets and suspicious of the other's motives. Yet their rivalry would also be the genesis of a world-leading partnership. Half a century later, Tate & Lyle would unite as a bold and innovative company, transforming the sugar industry and those who worked in it. Most notably, its refineries, on the River Thames in east London offered a new way of life for thousands of women – the so-called 'Sugar Girls'.

Women soldering the Golden Syrup tins in 1910

Above (clockwise from top left): Plaistow wharf, 1907; employees Agnes, Birdie and Alice in the factory laboratory c. 1900; an overview of the factory development laboratory, 1950; Lyle's employee, Jim Preston, c. 1900; an original syrup dispenser

Opposite: Advert from 1908

In the mid-1860s Henry Tate looked to London to expand his business. He settled on a huge derelict shipyard at Silvertown. By June 1878 the Silvertown refinery was up and running. In 1878 the refinery melted 214 tons of raw sugar; in 1899 his London and Liverpool Tate refineries were melting 2,000 tons of raw sugar per week.

When Abram Lyle set to work constructing a refinery – the famous syrup is a by-product of the cane sugar refining process – at

The Tate's Silvertown refinery pioneered the production of cubes rather than the traditional large conical blocks known as 'sugar loaves'. Cubes proved more convenient for grocers to store and were popular with customers.

Plaistow on the north bank of the Thames in 1881, among his neighbours, barely 1½ miles upstream at Silvertown, was Tate's refinery.

In business terms, Tate's sugar cubes didn't come close to Lyle's Golden Syrup, or 'Goldie' as it was known to employees. Records show that in 1914 only about a sixth of Lyle's 3,000-ton melt was turned into Goldie, while the rest was sold as conventional sugar. The profit on sugar, however, was only around £1 per ton, whereas Goldie fetched up to £6 per ton. Not bad for a by-product.

Lyle realised early in his Plaistow venture that his syrup would be a hit. Production was initially low-key - Goldie was poured into wooden casks and sold direct to employees or local residents in the know, but as word spread, so output rapidly increased. Within months, the refinery was selling a ton per week and casks were replaced by large 'Lyle's Golden Syrup' branded

LYLE'S GOLDEN SYRUP
IN 1lb. 2lb. 4lb. & 14lb. TINS
Abram Lyle & Sons Ltd London

dispensers and 1 lb and 2 lb tins for grocery store shelves. The Victorians couldn't get enough. As well as the definitive ingredient for steamed puddings, sponge cakes, pancakes and biscuits, it became fashionable in vegetable dishes, such as candied carrots or syrup dumplings.

In 1885, Goldie was sold in tins for the first time, a move that demanded an easily recognisable trademark to establish it as a trusted brand in the home. Lyle came from a religious family background, so it was perhaps inevitable that he chose a Bible story for the artwork. The illustration on the tins shows bees swarming around a honeycomb inside the rotting carcass of the lion killed by Samson. The accompanying quote from Judges 14 reads: 'Out of the strong came forth sweetness'. It's

not quite clear what Lyle had in mind. The reference to sweetness is obvious, but the debate continues as to whether 'the strong' referred to his company, Abram Lyle & Sons, or his robustly constructed tins.

By the turn of the century Lyle's Golden Syrup was a household name, its reputation enhanced by a simple advertising theme emphasising versatility and natural goodness. Poster adverts included the 'Inseparables', depicting two delivery boys – one from the baker's; one from the grocer's – walking arm in arm with a basket of freshly baked bread and an order of syrup tins (see opposite). Later, as rationing took a grip during the First World War, Lyle's posters assured the nation that their syrup was 'better than butter'. It certainly lasted

The recipe for Goldie was a fiercely protected secret (and remains unchanged to this day), there was a gentleman's agreement that Tate would not muscle in on syrup and Lyle would not sell sugar cubes.

Above: The original trademark design, which remains unchanged to this day

Right: A Model T Ford van used by Lyle's c. 1923 for delivering Golden Syrup

Opposite (clockwise from top left): Poster from 1913; poster c. 1900; black-and-white showcard c. 1900; poster c. 1913

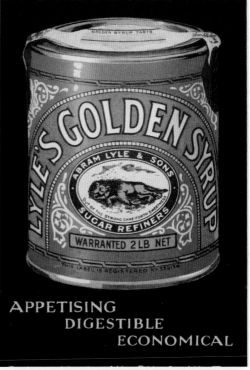

Above: Confectionery advert, 1898

longer. When the remains of Captain Scott's ill-fated 1910 Antarctic expedition were discovered by explorers in 1956, his supply of Lyle's Golden Syrup was found intact and perfectly edible.

The First World War brought new challenges for the Tate and Lyle businesses. For one thing, male employees were called up in their hundreds and had to be replaced by women – an unthinkable social change at the time. It heralded a new era in British manufacturing and many bosses feared productivity would suffer. In fact, refinery managers quickly realised their new employees were efficient and more than capable of working the punishing 12-hour shifts of physical labour.

One frustrating consequence of war was the government's control of sugar refining. Ministers imposed strict controls on profit, allowing refineries to bank only the same amount annually as their average over the three years prior to 1914. For Lyle's, perhaps the most worrying aspect of this was a ban on using tin. Metals were considered a vital resource for the war effort, certainly too vital for syrup, so Lyle's was forced to sell Goldie in cardboard canisters, with a rather sniffy explanation on the packaging (see below). In case syrup-lovers remained suspicious, the message concluded, in capital letters, 'LYLE'S GOLDEN SYRUP IS GUARANTEED PURE'.

Below left: Captain Scott's letter of thanks to the Lyle family, written in 1911 and despatched from the Antarctic, a tin recovered from the explorer's camp

Below right: The label on Lyle's Golden Syrup cardboard canisters during the First World War, when tin was requisitioned by the Ministry of Munitions, and one of the cardboard canisters

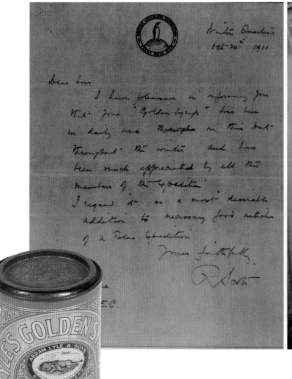

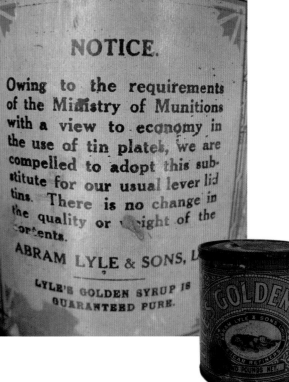

It was against this backdrop that, in the final years of the First World War, according to Antony Hugill in his book *Sugar and All That* (Gentry Books, 1978), Henry Tate's grandson Ernest approached Abram Lyle's sons Charles and Robert to consider a merger. This was itself an extraordinary act because there had been a long tradition of never speaking to each other. Senior family members went so far as to sit in separate carriages on the train to work from Fenchurch Street station. But now it was a case of needs must. The war had taken its toll on both companies and bitter rivalry had distracted them from foreign, subsidised competition, leaving little profit on their granulated sugar.

It took three years for the merger to go through but finally, in the spring of 1921, Tate & Lyle was born. The amalgamation was hailed a great success and when George V granted a royal warrant the following year, the company was quick to add the accolade to its tin design. More practically, with only one major buyer, there was less competition for raw sugar supplies. This in turn brought down prices at auction and helped increase profitability. Yet the management and workers at each refinery remained fiercely independent, describing themselves as working either at 'Lyle's' or 'Tate's'. As late as 1938 one manager from the Tate plant visited Plaistow to overhear a senior Lyle's executive insist that he was not to be shown the Golden Syrup process.

The outbreak of the Second World War was unquestionably the greatest threat to Tate & Lyle. But, like so many other British

Opposite: Tin-making at the Plaistow factory in 1949, and bulldog advert from 1935

These days, Lyle's Golden Syrup tins are filled at the rate of 240 per minute and more than a million are exported worldwide each year.

companies who manned the home front, the business came through with a fortitude and spirit that typified Britain's national pride.

For instance, men who were called up, provided they had been employed before the war, were paid an allowance to maintain their wage level (Tate & Lyle are thought to have been among the first major UK employers to take this step), and at each refinery up to 1,000 employees received training in fighting fires, first aid and rescue, while workers whose houses were bombed found their furniture removed for free by company vans. Dormitories for the homeless were set up alongside production lines and the company even laid on a hairdressing and beauty parlour for its army of women workers. For their part, employees took pride in arriving for work on time and looking smart; they were small, personal but hugely important acts of defiance during the war.

The end of the war saw Britain return to almost full employment. Despite this, unless women wanted a factory job, their work opportunities were limited to traditional trades such as domestic service, dressmaking or office work. However, women did want to work for Tate & Lyle. The company's two main refineries – Tate's Thames plant at Silvertown and Lyle's a mile upriver at Plaistow Wharf – were seen as excellent employers. It's not hard to see why.

The two refineries stood at either end of the East End's 'Sugar Mile', so called because Keiller's jam factory stood on the same stretch of the River Thames. All were competing to recruit and retain workers in a thriving east London economy and school leavers knew that if they didn't like one job they could simply stroll out and find another in the morning. Conscious of this, Tate & Lyle offered particularly attractive terms: top rates of pay, three lucrative bonuses per year and, most importantly, a ready-made social life. The Tate Institute included a subsidised bar and entertainment hall, with regular factory outings and sports days laid on.

Women – the Sugar Girls – signed up for Tate & Lyle by the thousands. There were plenty of opportunities for them: the massive packing operation on the Hesser Floor, the Blue Room, where sugar bags were made, or the tin-making plant for Lyle's Golden Syrup. All were dominated by female employees. It was hard, repetitive work and they were not expected to relieve the boredom by talking. Yet among these young,

feisty, independent East End women there was inevitably chatter and banter – even among the tin-makers, who coped with their deafening work environment by learning to lip-read. Lifetime friendships were duly forged.

By the late 1960s the Sugar Girls era was over. Machine technology replaced the need for a large workforce and the Plaistow refinery was wound down, its sugar refining buildings eventually demolished, though the factory making Golden Syrup remained. Workers were offered the chance to move down to the Thames plant at Silvertown, where sugar refinery continues to the present day.

Over the last half-century Tate & Lyle Sugars has remained one of the world's leading sugar refiners. Tate & Lyle Sugars' core values today – safety, integrity and respect – precisely sum up those espoused by Henry Tate and Abram Lyle when they first sold sugar in the late 19th century. The sense of public duty which the founders held so dear (Tate bequeathed much of his personal wealth to good causes and his collection of paintings formed the nucleus of what is now Tate Britain) still matters. And today in the very same way, of course, Lyle's Golden Syrup is made in the same Plaistow factory. Packaged in the same much-loved iconic tins. Poured slowly in all its mouthwatering majesty.

As the recipes in this book reveal, nothing else will do.

www.lylesgoldensyrup.com

Lyle's Golden Syrup holds a Guinness World Record for the oldest branding (packaging) for a brand in the UK. The same packaging has been maintained since 1885, with only slight technical changes during the war due to shortages of materials.

BREAKFAST
AND BRUNCH

PERFECT MORNING PORRIDGE

Piping hot porridge, served with Lyle's Golden Syrup, gets any day off to a great start. Put your Lyle's smile on every morning and that trusty glow will get you up and out – and the smile will last you all day!

Serves: 1

Prep: 2 minutes
Cook: 3 minutes, plus standing time

40 g rolled porridge oats
275 ml milk, or equal quantities of milk and water
Lyle's Golden Syrup, to serve

Combine the oats and milk (or milk and water) in a small non-stick saucepan over a medium heat. Bring to the boil, stirring continuously, and simmer for a couple of minutes until smooth and creamy.

Remove from the heat and leave to stand for 1 minute before pouring into a bowl.

Spoon or squeeze over a warming trickle of golden syrup and serve.

PORRIDGE TOPPINGS

Try any one of these delectable toppings on your warm porridge, after you've drizzled over the golden syrup.

- A sprinkling of ground cinnamon or freshly grated nutmeg

- A spoonful of your favourite jam

- A knob of butter

- Fresh berries, such as strawberries, raspberries or blueberries

- Chopped fresh apple

- Chopped dried fruit, such as raisins, prunes, cranberries, dates or apricots

- A sprinkling of toasted nuts and seeds (toast them briefly in a dry frying pan before serving), such as flaked almonds, chopped pistachios (see right), pumpkin seeds, sunflower seeds, flaxseeds

APPLE AND CINNAMON PORRIDGE WITH VANILLA AND ALMONDS

Porridge is a great way to start a wintery day. This one is extra special, flavoured with cinnamon, vanilla, ground nuts, seeds and apples.

Serves: 2

Prep: 10 minutes
Cook: 6 minutes

50 g rolled porridge oats

1 tablespoon mixed ground nuts and seeds, plus 1 teaspoon extra to serve

1 tablespoon ground almonds

15 g dried apple rings, chopped

pinch ground cinnamon

½ teaspoon vanilla bean paste or vanilla extract

200 ml unsweetened almond milk or whole milk, plus extra to serve

150 ml water

1 small eating apple, cored and coarsely grated or cut into small batons (skin on)

75 g piece peeled banana, sliced

25 g toasted blanched almonds, roughly chopped

Lyle's Golden Syrup, to serve

Put the oats, ground nuts and seeds, ground almonds, chopped dried apple, cinnamon, vanilla, milk and water into a saucepan over a medium heat and bring to the boil. Reduce the heat and simmer for 3 minutes, stirring occasionally, until the porridge is thick and creamy. Remove from the heat and stir in the grated or chopped apple, retaining some to decorate once served.

Spoon the porridge into bowls and top with the sliced banana, toasted chopped almonds, reserved apple and a sprinkle of ground nuts and seeds. Serve drizzled generously with the golden syrup, with extra milk to pour around the edge of the bowl.

CLASSIC PANCAKES

Why wait until Shrove Tuesday? Pancakes are endlessly versatile, and make a refreshing change from cereal and toast. These foolproof pancakes are hard to beat, and a drizzle of the nation's beloved 'Goldie' makes them purely irresistible.

Makes: about 8 pancakes

Prep: 5 minutes
Cook: 25 minutes

300 ml whole milk
2 eggs
125 g plain flour
25 g unsalted butter, melted, plus
    extra for frying
Lyle's Golden Syrup, to serve
lemon wedges, to serve

Put the milk and eggs into a jug or bowl and whisk together.

Put the flour into a large bowl, and make a well in the centre. Gradually pour the milk and egg mixture into the well, whisking continuously as you pour, until you have a smooth batter, then whisk in the melted butter.

Heat a non-stick frying pan (roughly 18 cm in diameter) over a medium heat, brush the pan with butter then pour in about 70 ml of batter, using a small ladle if you have one. Tilt the pan so that the batter covers the base of the pan evenly. Cook for about 1 minute, or until the batter has set and the pancake is golden underneath. Loosen the edges of the pancake with a spatula and give the pan a little shake – the pancake should come loose and move in the pan. Flip the pancake or turn it over with the spatula, then cook for a further minute. Continue to cook more pancakes in the same way, piling them up and keeping them warm once they're cooked.

Serve the pancakes with a drizzle of golden syrup and lemon wedges on the side.

Lyle's Tips

If you like, you can put all the ingredients into a food processor or blender and whizz until smooth, instead of mixing by hand.

If you have time, let the batter rest for 30 minutes – it improves the texture of the pancakes.

PANCAKE TOPPINGS AND FILLINGS

Keep it classic with lemon wedges, or get a bit more adventurous with one of these flavour combinations, using them to fill rolled pancakes or to top flat pancakes.

Blueberries and cream:

150 ml double cream

2 tablespoons Lyle's
Golden Syrup, plus extra
for drizzling

handful of fresh blueberries

Whisk the cream in a bowl until it forms soft peaks, then fold in the syrup. Spoon the sweet whipped cream onto the pancakes, scatter with blueberries and serve with an extra drizzle of syrup.

Nutty butterscotch sauce:

50 g unsalted butter

2 tablespoons Lyle's Golden Syrup

2 tablespoons granulated sugar

2 teaspoons cornflour

150 ml whole milk

150 ml single cream

handful of toasted pecan nuts,
chopped, to serve

Place the butter, golden syrup and sugar in a saucepan over a low heat until the sugar has dissolved, then let it simmer for 2 minutes. Blend the cornflour in a bowl with the milk and add 2 tablespoons of the hot mixture to the milk. Stir thoroughly, then pour the milk into the saucepan and bring to the boil, stirring until thickened. Remove from the heat and allow to cool slightly before stirring in the cream. Drizzle the butterscotch over the pancakes and scatter over the chopped pecan nuts to serve.

Chocolate nutty cream:

300 ml double cream

40 g chopped mixed nuts

25 g dark chocolate, grated

Whisk the cream in a bowl until it forms soft peaks. Spread the cream over the pancakes, scatter with the mixed nuts and grated chocolate and roll the pancakes, or serve them flat.

Orange sauce:

½ pint freshly squeezed orange juice

juice of 1 lemon

grated zest of ½ orange

4 tablespoons Lyle's Golden Syrup

½ teaspoon cornflour (optional)

3–4 tablespoons Grand Marnier
(optional)

orange segments, to serve

Put the orange juice, lemon juice, orange zest and golden syrup in a saucepan over a medium heat, bring to a simmer and reduce by a third. If the sauce is too thin, blend the cornflour with a drop of water and whisk it into the sauce to thicken. Finish with Grand Marnier, if using. Drizzle the orange sauce over the pancakes, adding orange segments to serve.

RICOTTA AND OAT BREAKFAST PANCAKES

Ricotta pancakes are popular down under and in the US. These ones are packed full of oaty goodness and will give you a great start to the day. Ring the changes with the fruits, according to what is in season.

Serves: 4–6
(2–3 pancakes per person)

Prep: 5 minutes, plus soaking time
Cook: 15–20 minutes

150 ml whole milk

25 g Lyle's Golden Syrup

1 teaspoon vanilla bean paste
   or vanilla extract

3 eggs, separated

1 tablespoon mixed ground seeds

100 g rolled porridge oats

1 teaspoon baking powder

150 g ricotta cheese

30 g unsalted butter, melted

To serve:

6 tablespoons natural full fat
   or Greek yoghurt

300–400 g strawberries,
   hulled and halved

Lyle's Golden Syrup

Whisk the milk, golden syrup and vanilla paste or extract into the egg yolks with a fork. Stir in the ground seeds, oats and baking powder and leave to soak for 15–20 minutes.

Break up the ricotta cheese with a fork and stir it into the oaty mixture with half of the melted butter. In a separate clean and grease-free bowl, whisk the egg whites until they form soft peaks and gently fold them into the ricotta and oat mixture with a large metal spoon.

Heat a large non-stick frying pan over a medium heat. Brush the base with a little of the remaining melted butter. Add 3–4 large spoonfuls of the batter, spaced well apart, to the pan and cook for 2 minutes on each side until they are golden brown and cooked through.

Serve the pancakes in batches as you cook them, or put them on to a plate, cover with a clean tea towel and keep warm in a low oven while you cook the remainder. Serve hot, topped with the yoghurt, strawberries and a drizzle of golden syrup.

Lyle's Tip

To keep the pancakes warm until you serve, put them on a heat-proof plate, cover with a clean tea towel and transfer to a low oven.

CLASSIC AMERICAN PANCAKES

Fluffy and light, this American breakfast and brunch staple has found a happy home in British kitchens over the decades, and nothing suits an American pancake better than a drizzle of liquid gold. Queen Elizabeth II even suggested, in a letter she wrote to Dwight Eisenhower in 1960 accompanying her own recipe for these 'drop scones', using golden syrup instead of sugar, as we do here.

Makes: 16 pancakes (serves 4)

Prep: 5 minutes
Cook: 25–30 minutes

3 eggs
4 level tablespoons Lyle's Golden
    Syrup, plus extra to serve
25 g unsalted butter, melted
300 ml whole milk
300 g self-raising flour
flavourless oil (such as sunflower
    oil), for frying

Beat the eggs, syrup and butter in a bowl until smooth, then whisk in the milk.

Place the flour in another bowl, make a well in the centre and gradually add the egg mixture, whisking continuously until you have a thick, smooth batter.

Heat a large non-stick frying pan over a low heat, and brush with oil. Spoon in a full tablespoon of the pancake batter, then add two or three more, leaving space between each pancake as they will spread a little in the pan. Cook over a low heat for 2–3 minutes, until small bubbles appear on the surface, then flip and cook on the other side until golden. Keep warm while cooking the rest of the pancakes (see tip on page 31).

Serve the pancakes warm, drizzled with extra syrup.

AMERICAN PANCAKE TOPPINGS

Quick and easy American pancakes make a perfect lazy breakfast or brunch dish. Serve them warm, with whatever takes your fancy, though you can't go far wrong with salty, crispy bacon, topped with a perfectly fried egg if you like, or a sweet and gently spiced apple compote.

Crispy bacon (see overleaf):

16 rashers streaky smoked bacon
   or pancetta
4 tablespoons Lyle's Golden Syrup,
   to serve

Grill or fry the bacon or pancetta until crispy, then drain on kitchen paper to absorb the excess fat. To serve 4, top a pile of 4 pancakes with a couple of rashers of bacon or pancetta and a drizzle of syrup.

Apple and cinnamon:

3 dessert apples, peeled, cored and
   cut into small chunks
1 tablespoon lemon juice
knob of unsalted butter
3 tablespoons Lyle's Golden Syrup
1 teaspoon ground cinnamon
dark chocolate, for grating (optional)

Put the chopped apples into a saucepan with the lemon juice and butter and cook over a medium heat for 2 minutes, tossing occasionally, until the butter melts. Add the syrup and cinnamon and simmer for 3–4 minutes, stirring, until the apples are tender and golden (stir gently, as you don't want the apple chunks to break up). Serve warm with the pancakes, topped with grated dark chocolate, if you like.

CHRISTMAS BREAKFAST MUFFINS

All the taste of Christmas, packed into a delicious breakfast muffin – perfect as a Christmas morning treat for the whole family, with an extra drizzle of syrup to make them even more decadent!

Makes: 12 muffins

Prep: 15 minutes

Cook: 20 minutes

85 g plain wholemeal flour

115 g plain flour

3 teaspoons baking powder

75 g demerara sugar

1 teaspoon ground cinnamon

½ teaspoon mixed spice

150 g dried cranberries

1 ripe pear, peeled

50 g unsalted butter

2 tablespoons Lyle's Golden Syrup

150 ml whole milk

1 large egg

Preheat the oven to 200°C/180°C fan/Gas Mark 6 and line a 12-hole muffin tin with paper cases.

Mix the two flours in a large bowl with the baking powder, sugar, spices and dried cranberries. Cut the pear into small dice and add to the bowl. Warm the butter and the syrup in the microwave for 1 minute, or in a small saucepan over a low heat, until the butter has melted. Stir together, then set aside.

Beat the milk with the egg in a bowl, then add it to the dry ingredients, along with the melted butter and syrup mixture. Stir until just combined (do not worry if there are a few lumps).

Spoon the mixture into the paper cases and bake for 20 minutes, until well risen and golden (a fine skewer poked into the centre of a muffin should come out clean).

Remove from the oven and transfer to a wire rack to cool.

Lyle's Tip

Dried sour cherries (not glacé) are a great alternative to dried cranberries, if you prefer them.

APPLE, GOLDEN SYRUP AND WALNUT MUFFINS

Chopped walnuts add a lovely crunchy texture to these sweet muffins, and the apple helps keep them extra moist. Using sunflower oil instead of butter helps them stay fresh for longer, so these will keep well in an airtight container for up to 3 days.

Makes: 12 muffins

Prep: 15 minutes
Cook: 18–20 minutes

300 g plain flour

3 teaspoons baking powder

1 teaspoon ground cinnamon

½ teaspoon mixed spice

50 g soft light brown sugar

50 g walnuts, roughly chopped

200 ml whole milk

5 tablespoons sunflower oil

1 large egg

1 teaspoon vanilla extract

2 dessert apples

3 level tablespoons Lyle's Golden
  Syrup, slightly warmed

Preheat the oven to 190°C/170°C fan/Gas Mark 5 and line a 12-hole muffin tin with paper cases. Alternatively, cut 12 x 10 cm squares of parchment paper and fit them into the tin holes, slightly overlapping the paper to take on the shape of the hole, and secure the base with a dab of butter to keep the paper in place.

Sift the flour into a large bowl and add the baking powder, spices, sugar and chopped walnuts, then mix together. Whisk the milk, oil, egg and vanilla extract together in a separate bowl. Peel and grate the two apples into the bowl with the flour.

Add the liquid ingredients and warm syrup to the dry ingredients. Quickly fold together with a large spoon or spatula, but do not over-mix.

Spoon the batter into the cases. Put the tray into the oven and bake for 18–20 minutes, until well risen and golden (a fine skewer poked into the centre of a muffin should come out clean).

Remove from the oven and transfer to a wire rack to cool.

Lyle's Tip

If the golden syrup is gently warmed through it becomes runnier and mixes more easily into the batter.

LAID-BACK BLUEBERRY MUFFINS

Easy. Quick. And oh-so tasty. These muffins make for a great breakfast treat – so start your day with a smile.

Makes: 12 muffins

Prep: 20 minutes
Cook: 25 minutes

For the muffins:

380 g self-raising flour
110 g Lyle's Golden Syrup
50 g golden caster sugar
175 ml vegetable oil
150 g Greek-style natural yoghurt
3 large eggs, lightly beaten
1 teaspoon vanilla extract
grated zest of 1 lemon
30 g rolled porridge oats
150 g fresh blueberries

For the topping:

1 level dessertspoon golden
   caster sugar
1 level dessertspoon rolled
   porridge oats

Preheat the oven to 180°C/160°C fan/Gas Mark 4 and line a 12-hole muffin tin with paper cases. Alternatively, cut 12 x 10 cm squares of parchment paper and fit them into the tin holes, slightly overlapping the paper to take on the shape of the hole, and secure the base with a dab of butter to keep the paper in place.

Sift the flour into a bowl and make a well in the centre. Add the golden syrup, caster sugar, vegetable oil, yoghurt, eggs, vanilla extract and lemon zest. Lightly and quickly stir everything together with a wooden spoon.

Using a metal spoon, fold in the oats and the blueberries (the mixture will be very thick and paste-like – this is fine). Divide between the cases, filling them almost to the top.

Mix the topping ingredients together and scatter the topping over the muffins.

Bake on the middle shelf of the oven for 25 minutes, or until golden and risen (a fine skewer poked into the centre of a muffin should come out clean).

Remove from the oven and transfer to a wire rack to cool. Hold off until ready to eat (this is the hard bit), then enjoy.

Lyle's Tip

These muffins freeze well, in a sealed freezer bag or container, if you're lucky enough to have any left over.

PEACH MELBA SMOOTHIE

Smoothies rely on well-flavoured fruit, so make sure your peaches are ripe and juicy, or plump for canned ones in fruit juice instead. Blood orange juice will give you a bright red smoothie.

Serves: 2

Prep: 5 minutes

3 large ripe yellow peaches
100 g fresh raspberries, plus 8–12
    extra to decorate (optional)
300 ml fresh orange juice
150 g Greek-style natural yoghurt
4 tablespoons Lyle's Golden Syrup,
    or to taste
handful of ice cubes

Put the peaches into a large heat-proof bowl or a deep saucepan, cover with boiling water from the kettle and leave for 30 seconds. Transfer them to a bowl of ice-cold water and, when cold, peel away the skins. Halve the peeled peaches and remove and discard the stones.

Put all the ingredients into a blender or liquidiser and blend until smooth. Alternatively, put everything into a measuring jug and blend with a stick blender, moving it up and down until everything is smooth.

Pour into chilled glasses, add a few ice cubes if liked, decorate with a few whole raspberries if you wish, and serve.

BANANA SMOOTHIE

Get the kids to help with this one: they'll certainly not mind doing a taste test! If you want a healthier version, leave out the ice cream and add more yoghurt.

Serves: 3

Prep: 5 minutes

4 bananas
60 ml orange juice
3 scoops vanilla ice cream, plus extra
    to serve (optional)
2 tablespoons Lyle's Golden Syrup,
    or to taste
3 tablespoons plain yoghurt

Peel the bananas, cut them into small pieces and put them in a blender or liquidiser. Add all the remaining ingredients and blend on full power for 20 seconds. Alternatively, put everything into a measuring jug and blend with a stick blender, moving it up and down until everything is smooth.

Pour into chilled glasses and serve with an extra scoop or two of ice cream, if you like.

DOUBLE CHOCOLATE MILKSHAKE

A delicious, easy-to-make drink that both children and adults will love.

Serves: 4

Prep: 5 minutes

80 g good quality dark chocolate
(minimum 70 per cent cocoa
solids), broken into pieces
500 ml ice-cold whole milk
200 g good quality chocolate
ice cream
2 tablespoons Lyle's Golden Syrup,
or to taste

Half-fill a small saucepan with water and bring to the boil. Place the chocolate into a small heat-proof bowl, sit the bowl over the pan of water, remove from the heat and leave to melt. Alternatively, melt the chocolate in the microwave in 20-second bursts (to make sure it doesn't burn). Leave to cool, then stir in half the milk.

Put the chocolate milk, chocolate ice cream, golden syrup and remaining milk into a liquidiser or blender and whizz until smooth. Serve in chilled glasses, with a straw.

Lyle's Tip

For a nutty twist, add a tablespoon of chocolate hazelnut spread to the blender before blitzing, or why not try replacing the dark chocolate with 40 g of your favourite chocolate bar.

FRENCH TOAST SANDWICH WITH PEACHES AND CREAM CHEESE

A popular brunch dish (and a great way of using up leftover bread), French toast can be made sweet or savoury. With juicy peaches and soft cream cheese, this sandwich version takes simple fried bread to a new level of deliciousness.

Serves: 1

Prep: 5 minutes
Cook: 5 minutes

2 large slices white bread
1 tablespoon cream cheese
8 peach slices, canned or fresh
1 egg, whisked
25 g unsalted butter
pinch caster sugar
Lyle's Golden Syrup, for drizzling

Spread one side of each piece of bread with the cream cheese.

Lay the peach slices on one slice of bread, on top of the cream cheese, and press the other slice of bread on top, cream cheese side facing down.

Dip both sides of the sandwich in the whisked egg.

Melt the butter in a non-stick frying pan over a medium heat. Pan-fry the sandwich in the butter until it is crisp and golden. Sprinkle with caster sugar. Slice in half, drizzle with golden syrup and serve.

FROZEN BERRY YOGHURT

This refreshing, ice-cold, fruity yoghurt takes just moments to make – perfect for putting a spring in your step on a hot summer morning.

Serves: 4

Prep: 4 minutes

4 tablespoons Lyle's Golden Syrup
500 g natural yoghurt
500 g mixed frozen berries
small handful fresh mint leaves
fresh strawberries, to decorate

Pour the golden syrup into 4 small chilled glasses.

Put the yoghurt into a food processor or blender with the frozen berries and blitz until thoroughly blended. Add the fresh mint leaves and blend again.

Spoon the mixture into the glasses, decorate with strawberries and serve.

Lyle's Tip

This recipe is endlessly versatile: try adding a few pieces of banana before you blend it and a grating of dark chocolate to finish, or scatter it with Granola (see page 49).

BIRCHER MUESLI

A great do-ahead recipe which can be made the night before. It will keep for a few days in the fridge. Also good served warm – just microwave the muesli before topping with the yoghurt and seeds.

Serves: 4

Prep: 15 minutes, plus soaking
  overnight
Cook: 1 minute

For the muesli:

185 g rolled porridge oats
275 ml apple juice
125 g natural yoghurt
1 tablespoon Lyle's Golden Syrup
1 red dessert apple, quartered
  and cored
1 green dessert apple, quartered
  and cored

For the topping:

1 rounded tablespoon flaked almonds
1 rounded tablespoon shelled
  pistachios, roughly chopped
2 tablespoons mixed seeds, such as
  sunflower, pumpkin, linseed, hemp
  and sesame
4 rounded tablespoons natural yoghurt
Lyle's Golden Syrup, to serve

Start by making the muesli: combine the porridge oats, apple juice, yoghurt and syrup in a bowl. Grate in both the apples, including the skins, and stir well. Cover and transfer to the fridge to soak overnight.

Just before serving, lightly toast the flaked almonds in a dry non-stick frying pan over a low heat for 1 minute. Add to the pistachios and mixed seeds.

Spoon three-quarters of the muesli into bowls, top each with a tablespoon of yoghurt, spoon over the rest of the muesli, scatter with the nuts and seeds, drizzle with golden syrup and serve.

Lyle's Tip

Try leaving out the apples, and scattering fresh chopped pears or figs over the muesli, just before serving. A few drops of vanilla extract in the muesli work well, too.

GRANOLA

Once you've made your own granola, you'll never look back. This is superior in every way to packaged varieties, not least because it's made just sweet enough with a generous dose of golden syrup. It's perfect scattered over yoghurt, served with milk, or sprinkled over a bowl of fruit compote.

Makes: 950 g

Prep: 5 minutes
Cook: 25 minutes

2 tablespoons vegetable oil, plus
    extra for greasing
150 g Lyle's Golden Syrup
1 teaspoon vanilla extract
200 g whole almonds
200 g whole pecans
200 g whole hazelnuts
250 g rolled porridge oats
sprinkling of ground cinnamon,
    to taste

Preheat the oven to 150°C/130°C fan/Gas Mark 2 and grease a large baking tray.

Mix the oil, golden syrup and vanilla extract in a large bowl. Add all of the remaining ingredients and mix well.

Tip the granola mixture onto the greased baking tray and spread it out evenly. Bake for 25 minutes until golden.

Once cooked, remove from the oven, cool, and store in an airtight container. It will keep well for up to 1 month.

Lyle's Tip

Add some seeds to the mix before baking, to boost the granola's nutritional content: try a handful of mixed sunflower, sesame, linseed and pumpkin seeds.

PASSION FRUIT AND MANGO GRANOLA POTS

These fruity little pots are great for breakfast or as a dessert after lunch or supper.
Assemble them just ahead of time, so that the granola stays nice and crunchy.

Serves: 4

Prep: 10 minutes
Cook: 3 minutes

25 g dried coconut flakes
100 g Granola (see page 49)
4 ripe and wrinkly passion fruit
1 small ripe mango
4 teaspoons Lyle's Golden Syrup,
    plus extra to taste
200 g Greek-style natural yoghurt or
    coconut yoghurt

Preheat the oven to 180°C/160°C fan/Gas Mark 4. Spread the dried coconut flakes out on a small baking tray and toast in the oven for about 3 minutes, until golden brown. Remove and leave to cool. Stir them into the granola.

Halve the passion fruit and scoop out the pulp into a bowl. Peel the mango and then slice the fruit away from either side of the flat stone. Cut 8 small, thin slices and set them to one side. Cut the rest of the fruit into small dice and mix into the passion fruit pulp. Stir in a little golden syrup to sweeten, if you wish.

Spoon the mango and passion fruit mixture into the bottom of 4 small glass tumblers or pots. Spoon on the yoghurt and then top with a layer of coconut granola. Drizzle over the golden syrup, decorate with the slices of mango, and serve.

SUPER-SEEDY FLAPJACKS

Pack one of these nutritional powerhouses into your bag or lunchbox for a satisfying on-the-go breakfast.

Makes: 12–16 flapjacks

Prep: 10 minutes

Cook: 25 minutes, plus cooling time

150 g unsalted butter

125 g soft light brown sugar

3 rounded tablespoons Lyle's Golden Syrup

grated zest and juice of 1 unwaxed lemon

75 g sesame seeds, toasted

50 g sunflower seeds

50 g pumpkin seeds

25 g golden linseeds

200 g rolled porridge oats

Preheat the oven to 180°C/160°C fan/Gas Mark 4 and grease and line a shallow 20 cm square tin with baking parchment or greaseproof paper.

Put the butter, sugar, syrup, lemon zest and juice into a medium saucepan and warm through over a low heat until the butter has melted and the sugar has dissolved.

Remove the pan from the heat and stir in the seeds and oats. Spoon the mixture into the prepared tin, pressing it firmly with the back of the spoon to level it out. Bake for 25 minutes, or until just golden around the edges.

Remove from the oven and leave to cool for 10 minutes, then cut into 12–16 pieces in the tin, while still warm. When completely cool, turn out the flapjacks to serve.

Lyle's Tips

Add finely chopped dried fruit to the mix in step 2 if you like.

The flapjacks keep well in an airtight container for up to 3 days.

SAVOURIES

GORGEOUS GLAZED RIBS

Glaze pork ribs with this indulgent treacly topping, which works perfectly in the oven or on the barbecue grill. Dig in and get sticky fingers...

Serves: 2

Prep: 10 minutes
Cook: 25–30 minutes

For the meat:

500 g pork loin rack of ribs
1 sprig fresh rosemary
1 large sprig fresh thyme
1 large clove garlic, unpeeled

For the glaze:

1 tablespoon Lyle's Golden Syrup
2 tablespoons tomato ketchup
1 tablespoon light soy sauce
1 rounded tablespoon soft dark
   brown sugar

Preheat the oven to 200°C/180°C fan/Gas Mark 6.

Place the ribs in a large saucepan and cover with boiling water. Drop in the rosemary, thyme and garlic clove and bring to the boil. Boil for 10 minutes, then drain and discard the water, herbs and garlic.

Pour the ingredients for the glaze into a small saucepan over a medium heat, then simmer for 3–4 minutes, until reduced and nicely sticky. Remove from the heat.

Transfer the blanched ribs to a baking tray and brush all over with the glaze. Pop the tray on the middle shelf of the oven and cook the ribs for 10–15 minutes, until the pork is completely cooked through and nicely sticky.

Place the barbecued ribs on a chopping board, slice into 'soldiers' and serve.

Lyle's Tip

Serve with a vibrant coleslaw, baked potatoes or corn on the cob, and plenty of napkins!

BARBECUED PORK CHOPS

Succulent pork works so well on the barbecue, especially when it's liberally basted with this moreish glaze, but these chops are equally delicious baked in the oven if the weather lets you down.

Serves: 4

Prep: 15 minutes
Cook: 40 minutes

4 large pork chump chops,
　trimmed of fat
1 tablespoon vegetable oil (if baking)
1 small onion, chopped (if baking)
salt and freshly ground black pepper

For the glaze:

2 rounded tablespoons Lyle's
　Golden Syrup
2 tablespoons light soy sauce
3 tablespoons tomato purée
1 clove garlic, crushed
½ teaspoon English mustard powder
juice of 1 large orange
juice of ½ lemon
1 tablespoon white wine vinegar

Preheat the oven to 180°C/160°C fan/Gas Mark 4, or heat the barbecue and leave it until it reaches a medium heat – a gas barbecue will take about 10 minutes but a charcoal one could take anything up to 30 minutes. When it is ready, the coals should be covered in a layer of light grey ash.

Season the chops generously. In a bowl, mix together the golden syrup, soy sauce, tomato purée, garlic, mustard powder, fruit juices and vinegar.

Turn off the central gas burners or rearrange the coals on the barbecue so that they lie around the edge of the grate, leaving a space clear in the centre. Place the chops on the barbecue grill and cook for 20-30 minutes, basting them frequently with the glaze, until they are cooked through. Alternatively, heat the oil in a frying pan over a medium heat and fry the chops quickly on both sides until browned. Remove them from the pan and place in a shallow ovenproof dish with the glaze and the onion. Cover with foil and cook in the oven for 30-40 minutes, until tender.

STICKY CHICKEN DRUMSTICKS

Serve these lip-smackingly tasty glazed drumsticks hot or cold, with a fresh green salad. If you prefer, you can cook them on the barbecue, but be sure to remove excess marinade from the chicken before placing on the grill, to avoid flare-ups.

Serves: 4

Prep: 10 minutes, plus
   marinating overnight
Cook: 30–35 minutes

8 chicken drumsticks

For the marinade:

3 tablespoons tomato ketchup
2 tablespoons light soy sauce
2 teaspoons Lyle's Golden Syrup
2 tablespoons fresh lemon juice
1 tablespoon sunflower oil
dash Worcestershire sauce
salt and freshly ground black pepper

To make the marinade, mix together the tomato ketchup, soy sauce, golden syrup, lemon juice, sunflower oil and Worcestershire sauce in a shallow dish and season with salt and pepper.

Carefully cut 3 slashes into the flesh of each drumstick then add them to the dish and coat them in the marinade. Cover and leave in the fridge to marinate overnight.

Preheat the oven to 190°C/170°C fan/Gas Mark 5. Line a roasting tin with foil and, using tongs, remove the chicken drumsticks from the marinade and place them in the tin. Bake in the oven for 30–35 minutes, until cooked through.

While the chicken is baking, transfer the remaining marinade to a saucepan over a medium–high heat and boil to reduce by half, basting the chicken with the marinade mixture every 10 minutes.

Lyle's Tip

You can swap the drumsticks for chicken thighs. To check if the chicken is cooked through, cut into the thickest part right to the bone – the juices should run clear.

TERIYAKI SALMON WITH SESAME SEED NOODLES

Teriyaki is a sweet and savoury glaze, popular in Japan, used most often with chicken and fish. It is simple to make, and gives a beautiful burnished mahogany colour to the finished dish.

Serves: 4

Prep: 5 minutes
Cook: 8–10 minutes

4 x 150–200 g skinless, boneless
    salmon fillets
4 teaspoons sunflower oil
2 spring onions, halved and finely
    shredded, to garnish
steamed bok choi, to serve

For the teriyaki glaze:

4 tablespoons tamari or Japanese
    dark soy sauce
2 tablespoons Lyle's Golden Syrup
4 tablespoons sake or Chinese
    rice wine
4 tablespoons mirin

For the sesame seed noodles:

250–300 g dried soba (buckwheat)
    or medium egg noodles
4 teaspoons toasted sesame oil
2 tablespoons toasted sesame seeds
pinch salt

For the teriyaki glaze, put the tamari or soy sauce and golden syrup in a small saucepan and stir over a low heat until the syrup has melted. Remove from the heat and stir in the sake or Chinese rice wine and mirin. Bring a pan of salted water to the boil for the noodles.

Add the salmon fillets to the glaze and turn them so they're completely covered. Heat the sunflower oil in a non-stick frying pan over a high heat. Add the salmon and cook for 2–3 minutes on each side until richly golden and just cooked through, then remove from the pan and leave to rest. Return the pan to the heat, add the remaining glaze and simmer briefly until reduced and thickened slightly. Take care not to let it catch and burn. Transfer to a heat-proof dish or bowl.

Drop the noodles into the boiling water and cook for 4 minutes, or until just tender. Drain the noodles well and toss in the frying pan with the sesame oil, toasted sesame seeds and a little salt.

Brush the salmon with the thickened glaze and pile the noodles alongside the salmon. Garnish with the shredded spring onions, and serve with steamed bok choi.

GRIDDLED THAI PRAWN SKEWERS

Fragrant and juicy Thai grilled prawns with a ginger kick make a refreshing change from burgers and sausages, and they cook in just a few minutes. Add a chopped red chilli to the marinade if you fancy a bit of heat.

Serves: 4 as a starter

Prep: 5 minutes, plus soaking and
    marinating time
Cook: 5 minutes

24 raw prawns
lime wedges, to serve

For the marinade:

1 tablespoon peeled and grated
    fresh root ginger
1 tablespoon light soy sauce
1 tablespoon Lyle's Golden Syrup
1 clove garlic, crushed
2 tablespoons finely chopped fresh
    coriander, plus extra leaves to
    garnish
grated zest and juice of 2 limes

To make the marinade, combine the ginger, soy sauce, golden syrup, garlic, chopped coriander and the lime zest and juice in a bowl. Place the prawns in the marinade, cover and chill for 30 minutes, until you are ready to start cooking. (Avoid marinating them for longer, or the acid in the lime juice will 'cook' the prawns.)

Thread the marinated prawns onto skewers (see tip) and cook over a hot barbecue, on a hot griddle pan or under a hot grill for 2 minutes on each side, until cooked through and a little blackened. Garnish with coriander and serve immediately, with lime wedges for squeezing.

Lyle's Tip

If you are using bamboo or wooden skewers soak them in water for 1½ hours before threading on the prawns, so that they don't burn during cooking.

VEGETABLE KEBABS WITH ORANGE SYRUP GLAZE

Use any combination of vegetables that you like for these kebabs. Sweet potatoes, aubergines and corn on the cob work well.

Serves: 4

Prep: 15 minutes
Cook: 25 minutes

For the kebabs:

350 g butternut squash, peeled and
   cut into 2.5 cm chunks
1 small red pepper, deseeded and cut
   Into 2.5 cm chunks
1 small yellow pepper, deseeded and
   cut into 2.5 cm chunks
3 small red onions, cut into wedges
2 small courgettes, cut into 1 cm
   thick slices
2 tablespoons olive oil
salt and freshly ground black pepper

For the orange syrup glaze:

juice of 4 large oranges (about
   400 ml)
4 tablespoons Lyle's Golden Syrup
4 tablespoons unsalted butter
2 teaspoons grainy mustard
4 cloves garlic, crushed

For the orange syrup glaze, boil the orange juice in a small saucepan until reduced to about 100 ml. Add the golden syrup and simmer until thick and glossy. Stir in the butter and, when melted, add the mustard, garlic and season to taste.

Put the squash, peppers, onions and courgettes in a bowl, toss with the olive oil and season with salt and pepper.

Thread the vegetables alternately onto metal skewers. Barbecue directly over a medium heat for 15–20 minutes until tender, then brush with the glaze and continue to cook, turning and brushing with more glaze, for about 4 minutes, until nicely caramelised.

ROAST PARSNIPS WITH STICKY WHOLEGRAIN MUSTARD GLAZE

The sweet and spicy glaze complements perfectly the starchy sweetness of these parsnips, which make an ideal accompaniment for a roast beef dinner.

Serves: 6

Prep: 10 minutes
Cook: 45 minutes

1.25 kg parsnips, topped and tailed, peeled, halved widthways and the thicker half cut into 2 pieces
200 ml sunflower oil
salt and freshly ground black pepper

For the sticky wholegrain mustard glaze:

4 tablespoons Lyle's Golden Syrup
4 tablespoons wholegrain Dijon mustard
2 teaspoons cider vinegar

Preheat the oven to 220°C/200°C fan/Gas Mark 7.

Drop the parsnips into a saucepan of salted boiling water and cook for 5 minutes. Drain well.

Pour the oil into a large roasting tin in which the parsnips can lie in a single layer. Put the roasting tin in the oven to heat up for 5 minutes.

Remove the tin from the oven, add the parsnips and toss them until they are well coated in the oil. Pour away the excess oil from the tin, season the parsnips with salt and pepper and roast for 30–35 minutes, turning them over halfway through so that they brown evenly.

Meanwhile, mix the golden syrup with the mustard and cider vinegar. Remove the tin of parsnips from the oven and brush them liberally with the glaze. Return to the oven for 5–6 minutes, or until golden brown and sticky.

Lyle's Tip

Try adding wedges of red onion, carrots or squash to the roasting tin with the parsnips – they all work well with this sticky glaze.

BARBECUED CORN ON THE COB WITH SWEET CHIPOTLE CHILLI GLAZE

You can make this recipe with cobs of corn still in their husks, or cobs already prepared. You'll just need to wrap them in foil if they are without their natural casing, before cooking, to stop the kernels burning over the heat.

Serves: 4

Prep: 15 minutes, plus
   soaking (if grilling with husks)
Cook: 25 minutes

8 sweetcorn cobs, ideally with their husks still intact
salt and freshly ground black pepper

For the sweet chipotle chilli glaze:

100 g unsalted butter, at room temperature, for spreading
250 g Lyle's Golden Syrup
4 cloves garlic, crushed
8 teaspoons chipotle chilli paste (or 4 canned chipotle chillies in adobo sauce, puréed)

Soak the sweetcorn cobs, if the husks are intact, in a bucket of cold water for at least 1 hour.

Drain the cobs (if they've been soaked) and carefully peel back the outer leaves, leaving them still attached at the base. Pull away and discard the silky strands, spread the ears of corn with butter then sprinkle with salt. Pull the husks back and tie them together at the tops with fine string or a length of the husk, to keep them in place while they are cooking. For peeled cobs, spread them with a little butter, season with salt and seal well in foil.

Heat the barbecue and leave it until it reaches a medium heat – a gas barbecue will take about 10 minutes but a charcoal one could take anything up to 30 minutes. When it is ready, the coals should be covered in a layer of light grey ash. Turn off the central gas burners or rearrange the coals so that they lie around the edge of the grate, leaving a space clear in the centre. Place the cobs side by side in the centre of the barbecue and cook over the indirect heat for 20 minutes, turning every 5 minutes, until tender.

Meanwhile, put the ingredients for the sweet chipotle chilli glaze in a small saucepan and simmer for 5 minutes until thick and syrupy. Remove from the heat.

Remove the sweetcorn from the grate and pull away the husks or foil. Brush generously with some of the chipotle chilli glaze, return to the barbecue (tying back the husks if necessary), and cook over a direct, high heat for about 4 minutes, turning, and brushing with more glaze, until they are lightly browned all over. Remove to a warmed serving plate, brush with some more of the glaze and serve.

SAUSAGE ROCKETS

You can't go wrong with these fun party treats: kids will love them, and grown-ups will try to pretend they don't! The soy and syrup glaze works well for any meat – add some Dijon mustard to the glaze if you fancy giving the rockets a bit of fire.

Makes: 8 'rockets'

Prep: 20 minutes
Cook: 20–25 minutes

8 large sausages
1 teaspoon light soy sauce
2 teaspoons Lyle's Golden Syrup
225 g ready-rolled all-butter
   puff pastry
1 egg, beaten, to glaze
sesame seeds, for sprinkling
2 red or yellow peppers (or 1 of each),
   halved and deseeded

Fry or grill the sausages until golden all over and cooked through, then remove and leave to cool. Preheat the oven to 220°C/ 200°C fan/Gas Mark 7 and line a baking sheet with baking parchment or greaseproof paper.

Push a wooden skewer through the middle of each sausage, from end to end. Place on a plate. Mix the soy sauce and golden syrup in a bowl then brush the mixture all over the sausages.

Unwrap the pastry onto a work surface and cut it into 8 long, thin strips. Wrap the pastry strips around the sausages in spiral form, taking care not to stretch the pastry, then place on the lined baking sheet. Brush the pastry with the egg wash, then sprinkle with sesame seeds. Transfer to the oven and bake for 12–15 minutes, until crisp and golden.

Cut triangle shapes from the pepper halves and push them onto the tips of the skewers, to finish (to resemble rocket fire).

Lyle's Tip

*Serve the 'rockets' with a tomato ketchup dip,
a creamy mustard dip, or one of the dipping sauces on page 73.*

SPECIAL SOY CHICKEN

Treat everyday chicken breasts to this great syrup twist on a soy sauce marinade. It couldn't be simpler. Try the marinade on chicken wings and thighs, too, or use it as a meat glaze when you're barbecuing.

Serves: 4

Prep: 10 minutes, plus
   marinating time
Cook: 20–25 minutes

4 skinless chicken breasts

For the marinade:

175 ml light soy sauce
125 g Lyle's Golden Syrup
2 teaspoons toasted sesame oil
4 cm piece root ginger, peeled
   and finely grated
freshly ground black pepper, to taste

Preheat the oven to 180°C/160°C fan/Gas Mark 4 and line a baking tray with baking parchment or greaseproof paper.

Combine the soy sauce, golden syrup, sesame oil, ginger and a generous amount of black pepper in a shallow non-metallic dish. Add the chicken breasts, cover and leave to marinate for a minimum of 2 hours (or ideally in the fridge overnight), turning from time to time.

Transfer the chicken to the lined baking tray, retaining the marinade for later. Bake in the oven for 20–25 minutes, or until golden brown and cooked through. Baste halfway through with the leftover marinade.

Transfer to plates and serve.

MARINADES

A marinade is a mixture of ingredients to which meat and fish are added before cooking. They usually include an acidic ingredient such as lemon juice or vinegar, which acts as a tenderiser, and oil, which helps to keep the meat or fish moist. They also add lots of flavour and are useful for using as a baste during cooking.

Sweet chilli marinade:

6 teaspoons sweet chilli sauce
2 tablespoons Lyle's Golden Syrup
3 tablespoons tomato ketchup
1 tablespoon red wine vinegar
1 tablespoon Worcestershire sauce
1 tablespoon sunflower oil

Great for chicken wings or drumsticks.

Combine all of the ingredients in a bowl and mix with your chosen meat. Cover and leave to marinate in the fridge for at least 2 hours, but preferably overnight. If using the marinade for fish, such as salmon fillets, only let the fish marinate in the mixture for 10–15 minutes.

Black treacle marinade:

2 cloves garlic, crushed
2 tablespoons red wine vinegar
2 tablespoons Lyle's Black Treacle
1 tablespoon Lyle's Golden Syrup
2 tablespoons tomato ketchup

Pork ribs are the perfect partner for this rich, dark marinade.

Combine all of the ingredients in a small saucepan and warm through over a low heat, stirring, until the treacle and syrup become runny. Remove from the heat and leave to cool, then mix with your chosen meat, cover and leave to marinate for at least 2 hours but preferably overnight.

Japanese soy and ginger marinade (see opposite):

2 tablespoons light soy sauce
thumb-sized piece root ginger, peeled and grated or cut into thin batons
1 tablespoon Lyle's Golden Syrup
2 tablespoons mirin
freshly squeezed juice of 1 lemon
lime wedges, to serve

Salmon fillets work beautifully with this sweet and sour marinade.

Whisk all of the ingredients in a bowl and add your chosen meat or fish. Cover and leave to marinate in the fridge for at least 2 hours, but preferably overnight. If using the marinade for fish, such as salmon fillets, only let the fish marinate in the mixture for 10–15 minutes.

GLAZES

A glaze is a combination of ingredients that usually contains sugar, honey or golden syrup, which is brushed onto the exterior surface of the food during and at the end of cooking. It caramelises over the heat, adding colour and flavour during cooking, and gives the food a glossy, sticky finish.

Soy butter glaze:

4 tablespoons melted unsalted butter

4 tablespoons light olive oil

4 tablespoons dark soy sauce

2 tablespoons Lyle's Golden Syrup

4 cloves garlic, crushed

salt and freshly ground black pepper,
   to taste

This makes a great alternative to the chipotle glaze for grilled corn on the cob (see page 67), and is also great for beef, salmon, chicken or tuna.

Combine all the ingredients in a saucepan and warm through. Remove from the heat and use to baste and glaze your chosen ingredient while it cooks.

Mustard glaze:

2 tablespoons wholegrain mustard

2 tablespoons Worcestershire sauce

2 tablespoons light soy sauce

2 tablespoons Lyle's Golden Syrup

pinch ground cloves (optional)

1 teaspoon freshly ground black
   pepper

Try using this to give pork chops, sausages or a roast ham a moreish golden sheen, or for roast parsnips or sweet potato wedges.

Whisk all the ingredients together in a bowl. Use to baste and glaze your chosen ingredient while it cooks.

DIPPING SAUCES

Dipping sauces are ideal for serving with barbecued fish, meat and vegetables, or finger food. The first two below can be used as dressings too, for vibrant Asian salads.

Chilli dipping sauce:

40 g light muscovado sugar

50 g Lyle's Golden Syrup

50 g caster sugar

60 ml dark soy sauce

30 ml cider vinegar

1½ teaspoons finely grated ginger

3 red chillies, deseeded and finely
  chopped

A thick, sweet and spicy dipping sauce, which is perfect with grilled chicken or vegetables.

Put all the ingredients in a saucepan and slowly bring to the boil, stirring to dissolve the sugar and the syrup.

Simmer for 15 minutes, until thick and syrupy, then tip into a bowl and leave to cool.

Thai Chang Mai dipping sauce:

6 tablespoons rice wine vinegar

4 tablespoons Lyle's Golden Syrup

1 clove garlic, finely chopped

2 thin slices ginger, finely chopped

1 red chilli, deseeded and finely chopped

1 teaspoon chopped fresh coriander

1 spring onion, very finely sliced

This light sweet and sour sauce is great for barbecued meats, prawns, little Asian meatballs and crisp vegetable fritters.

Simply mix the vinegar and golden syrup together until the syrup has dissolved, then stir in the remaining ingredients.

Indonesian satay dipping sauce:

1 tablespoon vegetable oil

50 g finely chopped shallots

4 cloves garlic, crushed

1 red bird's eye chilli, finely chopped

1–2 teaspoons sambal oelek or sriracha
  chilli sauce

1 tablespoon Lyle's Golden Syrup

125 ml coconut milk

50 g crunchy peanut butter

50 g roasted peanuts, finely chopped

2 tablespoons lime juice

1 teaspoon Thai fish sauce

salt and cayenne pepper

This is a wonderful dipping sauce for hard-boiled quail eggs, barbecued chicken, pork or beef, raw vegetables, and cooked peeled prawns.

Heat the oil in a small frying pan. Add the shallots, garlic and bird's eye chilli and fry gently until soft and lightly golden.

Add the chilli sauce to taste, the golden syrup, coconut milk, peanut butter and 75 ml water and simmer for 4–5 minutes until thickened. Stir in the chopped peanuts, lime juice, fish sauce and some salt and cayenne pepper to taste. Remove from the heat and leave to cool.

LYLE'S BEANY GOULASH

This rich and filling stew is nutritious and a great winter warmer, served with chunks of crusty bread. If you're cooking for vegetarians, leave out the bacon – it will taste just as good.

Serves: 4–6

Prep: 10 minutes

Cook: 1 hour 10 minutes

1 tablespoon sunflower oil

2 onions, chopped

200 g diced smoked bacon
   or pancetta

500 g carton passata

150 ml chicken stock

420 g can red kidney beans,
   drained and rinsed

420 g can cannellini beans,
   drained and rinsed

1 red pepper, deseeded and chopped

2 tablespoons Lyle's Black Treacle

1 tablespoon Lyle's Golden Syrup

1 teaspoon smoked mild or hot
   paprika (according to taste)

1 tablespoon wholegrain mustard

Preheat the oven to 180°C/160°C fan/Gas Mark 4.

Heat the oil in a flameproof casserole over a medium heat, add the onions and cook for 3–4 minutes, stirring frequently, until softened. Add the bacon or pancetta and cook for a further 5 minutes until they begin to colour.

Stir in the remaining ingredients and bring to a simmer. Cover and bake in the oven for 1 hour. Alternatively, simmer on the hob, covered, for 40 minutes. Serve with garlic bread if liked.

Lyle's Tip

Add sausages to the goulash, if you like. Just brown them in a frying pan before adding them whole to the casserole with the onions.

SAVOURY CHICKEN PARCELS WRAPPED IN BACON

This fail-safe stuffed chicken is simple to prepare, yet looks impressive on the plate. The bacon drizzled with golden syrup not only helps keep the breast meat moist, but it makes the chicken parcels irresistibly moreish, too. Serve with a crisp green salad and steamed new potatoes.

Serves: 4

Prep: 15 minutes
Cook: 35–40 minutes

200 g full-fat soft cheese
2 tablespoons snipped chives
2 cloves garlic, crushed
2 spring onions, trimmed and
   finely chopped
4 skinless chicken breasts
12 rashers streaky bacon
Lyle's Golden Syrup, for drizzling
salt and freshly ground black pepper

Preheat the oven to 200°C/180°C fan/Gas Mark 6.

Put the soft cheese, chives, garlic and spring onions into a bowl, season with salt and pepper and beat together until thoroughly mixed.

Cut a slit along the side of each chicken breast, then open them out. Stuff each breast with a quarter of the cream cheese filling, then close to form a parcel. Wrap each parcel with 3 rashers of bacon, starting at the thin end of the breast. Secure each stuffed breast with a couple of cocktail sticks.

Transfer the chicken parcels carefully to a roasting tin, drizzle each parcel with a little golden syrup and cook in the oven for 35–40 minutes, or until crisp and cooked through.

Leave to rest for a few minutes, then remove the cocktail sticks and serve.

BEEF WITH GOLDEN SYRUP AND GINGER

Golden syrup and black treacle add depth, sweetness and warmth to this rich and comforting Asian-style braise. Spicy watercress works well with the rich beef.

Serves: 4

Prep: 15 minutes
Cook: 1½ hours

1 tablespoon sunflower oil
4 x 175 g beef braising steaks, cut into
   bite-sized chunks
1 teaspoon finely chopped fresh
   rosemary leaves
2 cloves garlic, crushed
2.5 cm piece root ginger, peeled and
   finely chopped or cut into batons
1 tablespoon light soy sauce
1 tablespoon Lyle's Golden Syrup
1 tablespoon Lyle's Black Treacle
150 ml beef stock
150 g button mushrooms, sliced
1 teaspoon cornflour
salt and freshly ground black pepper
handful watercress, to garnish
cooked white and wild rice, to serve

Preheat the oven to 170°C/150°C fan/Gas Mark 3.

Heat the oil in a frying pan and quickly sear the steak chunks on all sides. Remove the steak from the pan and transfer to a shallow ovenproof dish.

In a bowl, mix together the rosemary, garlic, ginger, soy sauce, golden syrup, black treacle and stock and season with salt and pepper. Scatter the mushrooms over the steak, then pour over the sauce mixture.

Cover the dish with foil and cook in the oven for about 1½ hours, or until the meat is tender. Lift the meat out onto a warmed serving plate, cover and keep warm. Transfer the mushroom sauce to a small saucepan.

Blend the cornflour with 2 tablespoons of cold water and whisk it into the sauce, then reheat until slightly thickened. Pour the sauce over the steak and serve with a white and wild rice blend and a watercress garnish.

CRISPY DUCK WITH FRESH PLUM SAUCE

Treat your family and friends to a feast with this homemade take on a Chinese takeaway classic.

Serves: 4–6

Prep: 20 minutes, plus cooling time
Cook: 1¼ hours, plus resting time

2 kg whole duck (giblets removed)
1 tablespoon Lyle's Golden Syrup
2 tablespoons light soy sauce
1 teaspoon Chinese 5-spice powder
Chinese pancakes, cucumber batons
    and shredded spring onions, to
    serve

For the plum sauce:

450 g fresh plums or damsons,
    halved and stoned
150 ml white wine
1 sprig rosemary
1 cinnamon stick, halved
1 tablespoon rice wine vinegar
2–3 tablespoons soft light
    brown sugar
salt and freshly ground black pepper

Preheat the oven to 200°C/180°C fan/Gas Mark 6. Place the duck skin side up on a wire rack and set the rack over the kitchen sink. Prick the flesh in several places with a fork then pour over a kettle full of boiling water; set aside in a cool place (not the fridge) for 30 minutes.

Meanwhile, make the plum sauce. Place the stoned plums or damsons, white wine, rosemary and cinnamon stick in a small saucepan and simmer gently for 30 minutes, until the plums are completely softened. Put the duck in the oven to roast for 45 minutes.

Mix together the golden syrup, soy sauce and Chinese 5-spice powder, brush over the duck and continue to roast for a further 30 minutes, basting occasionally with the glaze, until the duck is well cooked – for this dish the meat should be brown, not pink. Remove from the oven and leave to rest while you finish the sauce.

Pass the plum sauce through a sieve into a bowl then stir in the vinegar, sugar and salt and pepper, to taste. Spoon into small serving bowls. Using two forks, shred the duck meat away from the bones and pile onto a serving plate. Serve with cucumber batons, shredded spring onions, plum sauce and Chinese pancakes for rolling.

Lyle's Tip

The fresh plum sauce is just as delicious made with other fruit such as nectarines or peaches. If you don't have time to make it yourself, a bottle of shop-bought hoisin sauce makes a decent substitute.

BEETROOT AND GREEN LEAF SALAD

This salad is a moveable feast – the versatile sweet dressing will work with whatever salad ingredients you have to hand. If you prefer cooked beetroot, roast them whole, peel and cut them into wedges to serve.

Serves: 6

Prep: 10 minutes
Cook: 15 minutes

2 thick slices bread, crusts
    removed and bread cut into cubes
6 tablespoons extra virgin olive oil
grated zest and segments from
    1 orange
150 g raw beetroot
1 tablespoon good quality
    balsamic vinegar
2 teaspoons Lyle's Golden Syrup or
    Black Treacle
½ teaspoon medium curry powder
1 clove garlic, crushed
large bag salad leaves e.g. baby
    spinach, watercress and rocket
salt and freshly ground black pepper

Preheat the oven to 200°C/180°C fan/Gas Mark 6. Spread the bread cubes out onto a baking sheet and drizzle over half the oil. Sprinkle with half the orange zest, toss and bake for about 15 minutes, turning halfway through, until the cubes of bread are crisp.

While the croûtons are baking, peel and coarsely grate the beetroot into a serving bowl.

To make a dressing, whisk together the remaining oil and remaining orange zest with the vinegar, golden syrup or black treacle, curry powder and garlic, and season to taste.

Toss the salad leaves with the beetroot, orange segments and crispy croûtons. Drizzle over the dressing and serve.

CHICKEN AND BACON SALAD WITH MUSTARD DRESSING

This fresh yet substantial salad makes a great lunch dish, and is simple to put together. Grill the bacon until crispy, to add a crunch to the dish, and serve with crusty bread.

Serves: 4

Prep: 15 minutes

150 g baby leaf spinach

150 g cherry tomatoes, halved

1 ripe avocado, peeled, stoned
   and diced

2 cooked skinless chicken breasts,
   diced or shredded

8 slices smoked streaky bacon, grilled
   and broken into pieces

50 g blue cheese, broken into pieces

For the dressing:

1 teaspoon wholegrain mustard

1 teaspoon Lyle's Golden Syrup

1 teaspoon white wine vinegar

squeeze of lemon juice

1 tablespoon extra virgin olive oil

To make the dressing, mix the mustard, golden syrup, vinegar, lemon juice and olive oil together in a bowl.

In a large mixing bowl, mix the baby leaf spinach, tomatoes, avocado, cooked chicken, bacon and blue cheese with the salad dressing. Divide between 4 plates and serve.

DUCK WITH APRICOTS IN ORANGE SAUCE

This twist on classic Duck à l'Orange ramps up the sweetness with apricots and that magic ingredient – golden syrup. Use ripe apricots if they are available, halved and stoned. Serve with fresh, steamed greens and fluffy rice or couscous.

Serves: 4

Prep: 10 minutes
Cook: 25 minutes

1 teaspoon sunflower oil

4 duck breasts (skin on)

1 small onion, finely chopped

450 ml chicken stock

grated zest and juice of 1 orange

50 g ready-to-eat dried apricots,
    roughly chopped

1 tablespoon Lyle's Golden Syrup

2 teaspoons cornflour

2 teaspoons freshly squeezed
    lemon juice

salt and freshly ground black pepper

toasted flaked almonds, to garnish

Heat the oil in a frying pan and sauté the duck, skin side down, over a medium–high heat until golden brown, then turn over and brown on the other side. Lift out and when cool enough to handle, peel away the fatty skin. Pour away most of the fat from the pan then return the pan to the heat and gently fry the onion, until golden brown.

Add the stock, orange zest and juice, apricots, golden syrup and season with salt and pepper. Bring to the boil, return the duck to the pan, cover and cook gently for 15 minutes. Remove from the heat, lift the duck onto a warmed serving dish and keep warm while you make the orange sauce.

Blend the cornflour with 2 teaspoons of water and the lemon juice. Stir into the pan and bring back to the boil, stirring until thickened. Simmer for a minute, then spoon over the duck and serve sprinkled with the almonds.

TANGY SALAD DRESSING

Bring an added dimension to your salads with this ultra-simple dressing, perked up with that special Lyle's warmth. It's perfect with the Beetroot and Green Leaf Salad on page 80.

Serves: 4–6

Prep: 10 minutes

200 ml extra virgin olive oil
2 tablespoons Lyle's Golden Syrup
1 tablespoon white wine vinegar
1 rounded teaspoon Dijon mustard
salt and freshly ground black pepper

Mix the olive oil with the syrup in a clean jar, add the vinegar and mustard, screw on the lid and shake until combined. Season to perfection with salt and pepper, then drizzle over your salad and enjoy!

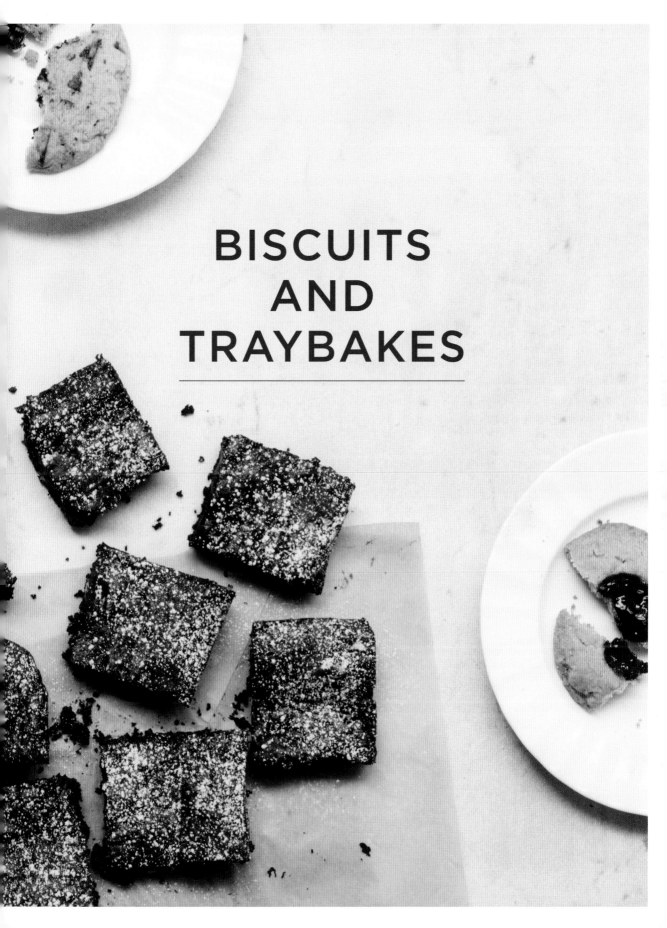

BISCUITS
AND
TRAYBAKES

CHEWY CHOCOLATE CHIP COOKIES

It's the golden syrup in these cookies that makes them extra chewy. Ring the changes with the chocolate if you wish. Milk chocolate or orange-flavoured dark chocolate are both very tasty alternatives.

Makes: about 14 large cookies

Prep: 10 minutes

Cook: 10 minutes, plus cooling time

225 g plain flour, plus extra
    for dusting

¾ teaspoon bicarbonate of soda

good pinch salt

120 g unsalted butter, at room
    temperature

100 g soft light brown sugar

75 g caster sugar

40 g Lyle's Golden Syrup

1 egg, lightly beaten

½ teaspoon vanilla extract

75 g good quality dark chocolate,
    roughly chopped

Preheat the oven to 180°C/160°C fan/Gas Mark 4. Line 2 large baking sheets with baking parchment.

Sift the flour, bicarbonate of soda and salt together into a bowl and set to one side.

Beat the butter, soft light brown sugar, caster sugar and syrup together for 5 minutes, until pale and fluffy. Gradually beat in the egg and vanilla extract. Fold in the flour mixture and chopped chocolate.

Break the dough into 14 even-sized pieces (about 50 g each) and roll them into balls with lightly floured hands. Place them onto the baking sheets and press down lightly, making sure there is 8 cm between each cookie. Bake for 10 minutes, or until lightly browned.

Remove the cookies from the oven and leave to cool on the trays for 10 minutes. Then transfer to a wire rack and leave to cool completely. Store in an airtight container.

GALLANT GINGERBREAD MEN

Is there anything better than a spicy gingerbread man? If you can't bear biting into these gallant chaps, this great mixture also makes lovely Christmas biscuits. You can bake them up to a month ahead and freeze, or make them up to 4 days ahead and store in an airtight container.

Makes: about 20 biscuits

Prep: 50 minutes
Cook: 10–12 minutes

For the gingerbread men:

350 g plain flour, plus extra
    for dusting
1 level teaspoon bicarbonate of soda
2 rounded teaspoons ground ginger
110 g unsalted butter, cubed,
    plus extra for greasing
175 g light muscovado sugar
1 large egg, lightly beaten
4 tablespoons Lyle's Golden Syrup

For the icing:

1 large egg white
175 g icing sugar
green paste colour (optional)

Place the flour, bicarbonate of soda and ground ginger in a bowl. Rub in the butter until the mixture forms fine breadcrumbs, then stir in the light muscovado sugar.

Make a well in the centre, stir in the egg and golden syrup and mix with a wooden spoon to make a soft, smooth dough.

Preheat the oven to 190°C/170°C fan/Gas Mark 5 and lightly grease 2 baking trays. While the oven warms up, turn the dough out onto a lightly floured surface and knead briefly. Roll out to 5 mm thickness and stamp out shapes with a 13 cm gingerbread man cutter. Transfer the gingerbread men to the greased trays, then re-roll the remaining dough and repeat.

Bake on the top and middle shelves for 10–12 minutes, swapping the trays halfway, until slightly darkened. Remove from the oven and leave for a few minutes to firm up, then transfer to a wire rack until they are completely cool customers.

For the icing, lightly whisk the egg white in a mixing bowl and gradually sift over the icing sugar. When the consistency is a bit like toothpaste (but tastier), divide the icing between two bowls, and add a little paste colour (if using) with a fine skewer to the icing in one bowl, mixing well. Spoon the plain icing into a piping bag fitted with a fine plain nozzle and ice buttons and bows on the gingerbread men, and faces if you like. If using, add green coloured icing to decorate. Leave to harden for a few hours before eating.

BRANDY SNAPS

You can't go wrong with classic brandy snaps, and they're only truly classic if they're made with golden syrup! Fill them with whipped cream just before serving, to make a decadent pud.

Makes: 10–12 brandy snaps

Prep: 20 minutes

Cook: 10 minutes

50 g unsalted butter, plus extra
    for greasing

50 g caster sugar

2 level tablespoons Lyle's
    Golden Syrup

60 g plain flour

1 teaspoon ground ginger

1 tablespoon brandy

finely grated zest of 1 lemon

Preheat the oven to 180°C/160°C fan/Gas Mark 4 and line a baking tray with baking parchment or greaseproof paper.

Place the butter, caster sugar and golden syrup in a saucepan and warm gently over a low heat until the butter and sugar have melted. Remove from the heat.

Sift the flour and ginger together into a bowl then stir into the melted mixture, along with the brandy and lemon zest.

Place small spoonfuls of the mixture on the prepared baking tray, well spaced apart to allow the mixture to spread. Bake for 8–10 minutes, or until bubbly and golden (the texture will be open and lacy).

Meanwhile, lightly grease the handles of three wooden spoons. Remove the biscuits from the oven and leave to cool for about 15 seconds. While they're still warm, gently loosen them with a palette knife and carefully wrap them - three at a time - around the wooden spoon handles with the lacy effect on the outer surface of the curl. If the biscuits are not flexible enough to curl round the handle, return the tray to the oven for 30 seconds.

Put the wooden spoons carefully on a wire rack and leave to cool, then gently remove the brandy snaps.

Repeat steps 4-6 with the remaining biscuits.

Lyle's Tip

To make brandy snap baskets, instead of shaping the biscuits around spoon handles, lightly press them around an orange while they are still warm and pliable, fluting the edges with your fingers. Leave to set and fill with whipped cream and fresh fruit to serve.

APPLE CINNY FLAPJACKS

These moreish fruity flapjacks are best eaten within 2 days of making (without the apple decoration). If you like, substitute the sunflower seeds with chopped toasted hazelnuts.

Makes: 12–16 flapjacks

Prep: 10 minutes
Cook: 30–35 minutes,
    plus cooling time

115 g unsalted butter
75 g demerara sugar
3 rounded tablespoons
    Lyle's Golden Syrup
250 g rolled porridge oats
1 teaspoon ground cinnamon
2 dessert apples, washed
2 tablespoons sunflower seeds

To decorate:

1 dessert apple
3 tablespoons Lyle's Golden Syrup

Preheat the oven to 180°C/160°C fan/Gas Mark 4, grease a shallow 20 cm square tin and line it with baking parchment or greaseproof paper.

Place the butter, sugar and golden syrup in a saucepan and warm gently over a low heat until the butter and sugar have melted. Remove from the heat. Stir in the oats and cinnamon and mix thoroughly. Grate the apples (with skin on) into the mixture, add the sunflower seeds and stir to combine.

Spoon the mixture into the prepared tin and press evenly and firmly with the back of the spoon to level it out. Bake for 30–35 minutes, or until golden.

Remove from the oven and cool for 10 minutes, then cut into 12–16 pieces while still warm.

To make the decoration, quarter the apple, remove the core and slice thinly. Put the golden syrup into a small non-stick frying pan, add the apple slices and cook them in the syrup over a medium heat for 3–4 minutes. When the flapjack is completely cool, turn out the individual flapjacks. Decorate each piece with syrup-soaked apple slices.

CRACKLE MALLOW FLAPJACKS

This is a great rainy-day bake for kids, and they can get creative with the decorations, too, adding Smarties or small pieces of toffee or edible glitter. The possibilities are endless!

Makes: 25 flapjacks

Prep: 20 minutes
Cook: 25 minutes,
    plus cooling time

125 g unsalted butter
50 g mini marshmallows, plus an
    extra handful for decorating
75 g caster sugar
3 rounded tablespoons Lyle's
    Golden Syrup
150 g rolled porridge oats
50 g Rice Krispies cereal

To decorate:

75 g icing sugar
100 g dark chocolate (minimum
    70 per cent cocoa solids)

Preheat the oven to 180°C/160°C fan/Gas Mark 4, grease a shallow 20 cm square tin and line it with baking parchment or greaseproof paper.

Put the butter, mini marshmallows, caster sugar and golden syrup in a saucepan and warm gently over a low heat until the butter and marshmallows have melted. Remove from the heat.

Stir the oats into the melted mixture until completely coated, then gently fold in the crispy cereal. Spoon the mixture into the prepared tin and press evenly and firmly with the back of the spoon to level it out. Bake for 25 minutes, or until just golden around the edges.

Remove from the oven (keep the oven on), top with the extra marshmallows, and pop back in the oven for 1 minute, until they have melted. Remove from the oven and leave to cool a little for 10 minutes, then cut into 25 pieces while still warm. When completely cool, turn out the individual flapjacks and place on a wire rack.

Mix the icing sugar with 2 teaspoons of cold water until smooth. Drizzle over the flapjacks. Heat the chocolate in the microwave in 20-second bursts until melted, then drizzle it over the flapjacks. Allow the icing and chocolate to set before serving.

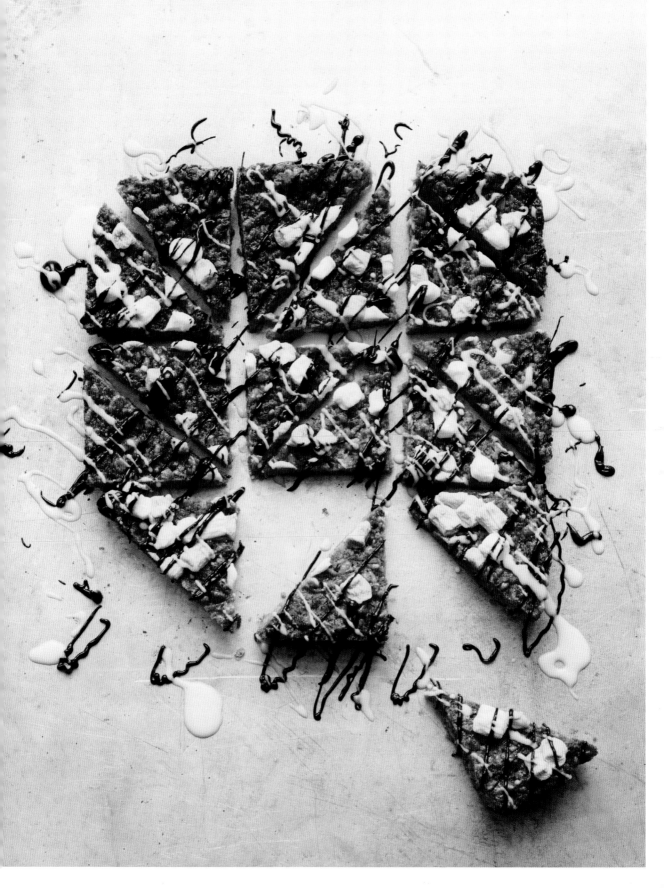

DOUBLE CHOCOLATE FLAPJACKS

To make these double chocolate flapjacks even more chocolatey, dip them in melted dark chocolate once cooled, then leave to set before serving. They're great fun to make with the kids.

Makes: 12–16 flapjacks

Prep: 10 minutes
Cook: 25 minutes,
    plus cooling time

175 g unsalted butter, plus extra
    for greasing
100 g soft light brown sugar
3 rounded tablespoons
    Lyle's Golden Syrup
225 g rolled porridge oats
30 g cocoa powder
100 g dark or milk chocolate chips
extra cocoa powder, to dust (optional)

Preheat the oven to 180°C/160°C fan/Gas Mark 4, grease a shallow 20 cm square tin and line it with baking parchment or greaseproof paper.

Place the butter, sugar and golden syrup in a saucepan and warm gently over a low heat until the butter and sugar have melted. Remove from the heat. Toss the oats and cocoa powder together in a bowl, then stir them into the melted mixture along with the chocolate chips.

Spoon the mixture into the prepared tin and press evenly and firmly with the back of the spoon to level it out. Bake for 25 minutes, or until just darkened around the edges.

Remove from the oven and cool for 10 minutes, then cut into 12–16 pieces while still warm. Leave to cool completely before turning out onto a board and cutting again with a sharp knife. Sift a little cocoa powder over the flapjacks before serving, if you like.

SALTED CARAMEL FUDGE FLAPJACKS

The combination of sweetness and saltiness works so well in these scrummy flapjacks. And best of all, they are really easy to make.

Makes: 20 flapjacks

Prep: 30 minutes
Cook: 35–40 minutes, plus
   chilling time

For the flapjack base:

**200 g salted butter, plus extra
   for greasing**
95 g Lyle's Golden Syrup
350 g rolled porridge oats

For the salted caramel fudge:

397 g can condensed milk
95 g Lyle's Golden Syrup
225 g soft light brown sugar
125 g unsalted butter
2 tablespoons liquid glucose
**175 g white chocolate, chopped
   into small pieces**
sea salt flakes, for sprinkling

Preheat the oven to 200°C/180°C fan/Gas Mark 6, grease a 30 x 18 cm shallow baking tin and line it with baking parchment or greaseproof paper.

To make the flapjack base, heat the butter with the golden syrup in a heavy-based saucepan over a medium heat until the butter has melted. Increase the heat and just as the mixture starts to come to the boil add the oats, mixing well with a wooden spoon. Remove from the heat. Spoon the mixture into the prepared tin and press evenly and firmly with the back of the spoon to level it out. Bake for 15–18 minutes, or until lightly golden. Remove from the oven and set aside while you make the fudge.

To make the salted caramel fudge, combine the condensed milk, golden syrup, soft light brown sugar, butter and liquid glucose in a heavy-based saucepan. Place over a low heat and cook for about 10 minutes, stirring frequently with a wooden spoon, until the sugar has melted. Bring to the boil then simmer for 8–10 minutes, stirring constantly, until the fudge has thickened and is light golden brown in colour.

Remove from the heat, add the white chocolate and stir until melted and the mixture comes together. Quickly spoon the fudge evenly over the flapjack base, place a sheet of greaseproof paper directly on top then place another tin of the same size on top of that and press down to level the surface. Lift off the paper and sprinkle the fudge lightly with sea salt flakes, rubbing the salt between your fingers to break up the flakes as you sprinkle. Lay the paper back down again, place the tray on top and gently press down to help the salt stick to the fudge. If you don't have another tin the same size, just quickly spread the fudge out with a palette knife, sprinkle with salt and lightly press the salt in.

Transfer the fudgy flapjack to the fridge to chill for 1–2 hours until firm. Cut into 20 rectangles, arrange on a plate and serve.

DUSTED CHOCOLATE BROWNIES

Gooey and rich, this is the ultimate chocolate brownie recipe. Be sure not to overcook the brownies, as you'll lose the delectably soft, fudgy centre.

Makes: 12 brownies

Prep: 15 minutes

Cook: 25 minutes,
   plus cooling time

150 g dark chocolate (minimum
   70 per cent cocoa solids)

115 g unsalted butter, plus extra
   for greasing

2 tablespoons Lyle's Golden Syrup

2 large eggs, beaten

few drops vanilla extract

115 g self-raising flour

50 g icing sugar, plus extra for dusting

25 g cocoa powder

50 g milk or white chocolate chips

Preheat the oven to 180°C/160°C fan/Gas Mark 4. Grease an 18 cm shallow square baking tin and line it with baking parchment or greaseproof paper.

Break the chocolate into a saucepan and add the butter and syrup. Warm gently over a low heat, stirring, until the chocolate and butter have melted. Remove from the heat and leave to cool slightly.

Stir the beaten eggs, vanilla extract, flour, icing sugar, cocoa powder and chocolate chips into the melted chocolate mixture, mixing until well blended, then transfer to the prepared tin and bake for 25 minutes, until set and covered in a flaky crust.

Remove from the oven, leave to cool a little, then cut into 16 squares and transfer to a wire rack to cool completely. Dust liberally with icing sugar and serve.

Lyle's Tip

Serve these brownies hot from the tin with a scoop of vanilla ice cream, Nutty Butterscotch Ice Cream (page 122) or a drizzle of cream to make a brilliant pudding.

RASPBERRY JAM DROPS

Buttery, sticky and sweet, these jam drops are perfect mid-morning pick-me-up morsels, and taste even better filled with homemade jam. They're easy to prepare, bake and eat, making them a firm favourite with kids and adults alike.

Makes: about 24 drops

Prep: 20 minutes
Cook: 15–20 minutes

175 g plain flour
25 g cornflour
½ teaspoon baking powder
175 g unsalted butter, at room
   temperature
50 g caster sugar
2 level tablespoons Lyle's
   Golden Syrup
1 teaspoon vanilla extract
4 tablespoons raspberry jam

Preheat the oven to 180°C/160°C fan/Gas Mark 4 and line 2–3 baking trays with baking parchment.

Sift the flour, cornflour and baking powder into a bowl.

In a separate bowl, beat the butter, sugar and golden syrup until pale and fluffy, then add the vanilla extract. Fold the sifted dry ingredients into the butter mixture until it forms a soft dough.

Take small pieces of dough, about the size of a walnut, and roll them into a ball. Place on one of the prepared baking trays, then repeat and make more balls, leaving room for them to spread as you place them on the trays.

Using your finger, make an imprint into each ball deep enough to hold a little jam. Carefully place a small blob of jam (about ¼ teaspoon) into each well.

Bake for 15–20 minutes, or until lightly golden brown, then carefully transfer to a wire rack to cool completely. They will keep in an airtight container for up to 4 days.

Lyle's Tip

You can use other flavoured jams or lemon curd in place of the raspberry jam.

CARAMEL CHOCOLATE SHORTCAKE

Our own special take on millionaire's shortbread, these crumbly, chewy rich bites look impressive yet are incredibly easy. To make them go further, cut them into 24 squares instead of 12.

Makes: 12 pieces

Prep: 25 minutes
Cook: 25–30 minutes, plus setting
   and chilling time

For the base:

125 g unsalted butter, at room
   temperature, plus extra for greasing
50 g caster sugar
175 g plain flour, sifted

For the filling:

125 g unsalted butter
50 g caster sugar
2 tablespoons Lyle's Golden Syrup
150 ml condensed milk

For the topping:

150 g dark chocolate (minimum
   70 per cent cocoa solids), broken
   into pieces

Preheat the oven to 180°C/160°C fan/Gas Mark 4 and grease a 20 cm baking tin.

Cream together the butter and sugar for the base in a bowl until light and fluffy. Sift in the flour and stir until the ingredients are thoroughly mixed. Knead until smooth.

Press the dough evenly into the bottom of the prepared tin and prick the surface with the prongs of a fork. Bake for 25–30 minutes, remove from the oven and leave to cool in the tin.

Meanwhile, place the filling ingredients in a saucepan over a medium heat and stir until the sugar has dissolved. Bring to the boil slowly, then simmer, stirring continuously for 5–7 minutes. Remove from the heat and leave to cool slightly, then pour over the biscuit base and leave to set.

For the topping, half-fill a small saucepan with water and bring to the boil. Place the chocolate in a small heat-proof bowl, sit the bowl over the pan of water, remove from the heat and leave to melt. Alternatively, melt the chocolate in the microwave in 20-second bursts (to make sure it doesn't burn). Leave to cool then spread it over the set caramel. Transfer to the fridge to set, then cut into 12 squares with a sharp knife.

PUDDINGS, TARTS AND DESSERTS

CHOCOLATE PECAN TART WITH CINNAMON CREAM

Smooth, rich and delicious, serve this very moreish chocolate tart with cinnamon cream or a scoop of vanilla ice cream on top.

Serves: 8

Prep: 35 minutes, plus chilling time
Cook: 1 hour, plus cooling time

For the pastry:

175 g plain flour, plus extra for dusting
125 g unsalted butter, chilled
    and cubed
20 g golden caster sugar
pinch salt
2¼ tablespoons cold water

For the filling:

75 g dark chocolate (minimum
    70 per cent cocoa solids), broken
    into pieces
40 g unsalted butter
225 g Lyle's Golden Syrup
150 g granulated sugar
3 eggs, lightly beaten
95 g pecan nuts

For the cinnamon cream:

150 ml double cream
40 g Lyle's Golden Syrup
½ level teaspoon ground cinnamon

To decorate:

25 g dark chocolate (minimum
    70 per cent cocoa solids), broken
    into pieces
icing sugar, to dust

To make the pastry, place the flour, butter, sugar and salt in a food processor and pulse until the mixture resembles fine breadcrumbs. Add the water and pulse until it comes together into a ball. Alternatively, sift the flour and salt into a bowl then rub in the butter until the mixture resembles fine breadcrumbs. Stir in the water to bring it together into a soft dough. Wrap the dough in clingfilm and chill for 30 minutes.

Meanwhile, make the filling. Melt the chocolate and butter in a saucepan over a low heat. Set aside. In another pan heat the golden syrup and sugar over a low heat for about 10 minutes, stirring, until the sugar dissolves. Bring to the boil, simmer for 2 minutes, stirring, then remove and leave to cool. Whisk the melted chocolate and butter into the eggs, followed by the syrup mixture, and set aside.

Roll out the chilled pastry on a lightly floured surface, then use it to line a 20 cm round tart tin. Lightly prick the base and chill for 30 minutes. Preheat the oven to 190°C/170°C fan/Gas Mark 5. Trim off any excess pastry, line the tart with baking parchment and fill with baking beans. Place the tin on a baking sheet and bake blind for 12 minutes. Remove the parchment and beans and bake for a further 5–6 minutes until the pastry is lightly browned. Remove the pastry from the oven and reduce the oven temperature to 180°C/160°C fan/Gas Mark 4.

Pour the filling into the case and bake for 20–25 minutes, or until a skin forms on the surface. Remove, arrange the pecans on top, and bake for a further 10–15 minutes, or until set. Remove and leave to cool for 1 hour.

Melt the chocolate for the decoration (see final step on page 100) then set aside to cool. For the cinnamon cream, whisk the cream to soft peaks, then marble in the golden syrup and cinnamon.

Lift the tart out of its tin, dust with icing sugar, then drizzle over the melted chocolate and serve with the cinnamon cream.

GOOEY CHOCOLATE AND PEANUT WHOOPIE PIES

The whoopie pie is a classic American dessert and sits somewhere between a cookie and a cake, with a filling in the middle – this one is creamy, crunchy and nutty.

Makes: 12 pies

Prep: 45 minutes

Cook: 8–9 minutes,
     plus cooling time

For the sponge:

95 g soft light brown sugar

125 g unsalted butter, cubed, softened

95 g Lyle's Golden Syrup

2 large eggs, at room temperature

275 g plain flour

2 rounded tablespoons cocoa powder

1 rounded teaspoon bicarbonate
   of soda

½ rounded teaspoon baking powder

120 ml buttermilk

For the filling:

165 g full-fat cream cheese

165 g crunchy peanut butter

75 g icing sugar, plus extra for dusting

Preheat the oven to 200°C/180°C fan/Gas Mark 6 and line 2 large baking trays with greaseproof paper.

To make the sponge, put the soft light brown sugar, butter and golden syrup in the bowl of a stand mixer and beat at high speed for 4–5 minutes until pale and creamy, scraping down the sides. Alternatively, mix in a bowl with an electric hand mixer.

Reduce the speed of the mixer and add the eggs, one at a time, then increase the speed and beat until well combined, scraping down the sides of the bowl so that all the mixture is well incorporated. Don't worry if the mixture is slightly curdled as it will emulsify once you add the flour mixture.

In a separate bowl sift the flour, cocoa powder, bicarbonate of soda and baking powder and mix together. Add a spoonful of the flour mixture and a spoonful of the buttermilk to the creamed mixture and fold in with a large metal spoon. Repeat until the flour mixture and buttermilk are thoroughly incorporated and the mixture has a thick spoonable consistency.

Divide the mixture between the baking trays using a tablespoon – you should get about 24 spoonfuls (12 on each tray), with each dollop about 6 cm in diameter, ensuring they are well spaced apart to allow the mixture room to spread. Bake on the top and middle shelves of the oven for 8–9 minutes, swapping the trays halfway through, until risen, nicely browned and the tops spring back when lightly touched. Remove from the oven and leave to cool briefly on the trays, then peel away from the greaseproof paper and transfer to a wire rack to cool completely.

Place the cream cheese and peanut butter in a mixing bowl, sift over the icing sugar and beat together until well combined. Divide the filling between half of the sponges, spreading it to the edges, then top with the remaining sponges and gently squeeze together. Lightly dust with icing sugar, arrange on a plate and serve.

BANANA SPLITS WITH EASY CHOCOLATE SAUCE

This simple chocolate sauce can be made in no time at all. It's so versatile and works with many desserts such as this sweet 'hot dog' made with brioche buns and beautifully caramelised bananas.

Serves: 4

Prep: 15 minutes
Cook: 5–7 minutes

For the chocolate sauce:

75 g dark chocolate (minimum
    70 per cent cocoa solids),
    broken into squares
25 ml whipping cream
25 g unsalted butter, cubed
25 g Lyle's Golden Syrup

For the banana splits:

2 small ripe bananas, peeled and
    sliced in half lengthways
25 g golden caster sugar
4 small brioche finger rolls
1 heaped tablespoon flaked almonds
icing sugar, for dusting (optional)
Lyle's Golden Syrup, for drizzling
4 scoops vanilla ice cream, to serve

Set a heat-proof bowl over a saucepan of simmering water, making sure the bowl doesn't touch the water. Add the chocolate, cream, butter and golden syrup and stir with a wooden spoon for 1–2 minutes, until the chocolate and butter have melted and all the ingredients are combined. Turn off the heat but leave the bowl over the pan, as the water beneath the bowl will keep the sauce warm.

Preheat the grill. Place the banana halves on a baking tray cut side up, sprinkle over the caster sugar and grill for 3–4 minutes, until golden and caramelised. Warm the brioche rolls through on a shelf below the bananas, while the bananas are cooking.

Place the almonds in a small, dry non-stick frying pan over a moderate heat and toast for 1–2 minutes, until lightly golden, stirring occasionally. Remove from the heat and dust lightly with icing sugar.

Cut the brioche rolls through the tops, just like a hot-dog bun, being careful not to cut all the way through.

To serve, open up the brioche rolls slightly, place a grilled banana half in each, drizzle over some of the warm chocolate sauce, scatter with the toasted almonds, dust lightly with icing sugar, if you like, and drizzle over some golden syrup. Arrange on a platter or individual plates and serve with the remaining chocolate sauce and the vanilla ice cream.

GOLDEN CHRISTMAS PUDDING WITH ORANGE BRANDY BUTTER

Here's a festive pudding that's full of golden goodness. It's the perfect way to round off Christmas lunch or dinner. Adorn the cooked pudding with frosted grapes if you like, to give it that extra festive touch. If you've got a lot on at Christmas you can make this pudding and the brandy butter a month ahead of time and freeze them in lidded containers.

Serves: 8

Prep: 15 minutes

Cook: 3 hours, plus 1 hour to reheat

115 g unsalted butter, softened, plus extra for greasing

115 g soft light brown sugar

2 eggs, at room temperature, lightly beaten

75 g self-raising flour

2 tablespoons Lyle's Golden Syrup

1 teaspoon ground cinnamon

¼ teaspoon freshly grated nutmeg

grated zest and juice of 1 small orange

75 g raisins

125 g sultanas

75 g ready-to eat dried apricots, chopped

75 g dried sour cherries or cranberries

50 g cut mixed peel

3 balls of stem ginger in syrup, drained and finely chopped

1 dessert apple, peeled and grated

75 g fresh brown breadcrumbs

Grease a 1.2 litre pudding basin and line the base with a small round piece of baking parchment.

Cream the butter with the soft light brown sugar in a bowl until soft and fluffy, then gradually beat in the eggs with a little of the flour. When the eggs have been added, sift in the remaining flour, and add the golden syrup and spices.

Add the orange zest and juice with the dried fruits, mixed peel, stem ginger and grated apple, and slowly stir in the breadcrumbs: the mixture should have a soft dropping consistency.

Turn the pudding mix into the prepared pudding basin and smooth the top. Pleat a circle of baking parchment and foil (cut two times larger than the diameter of the top of the pudding basin) by folding over 2.5 cm in the centre. This will allow for the pudding to expand as it cooks. Cover the basin with the parchment, with the pleat in the centre of the pudding, then cover with the foil, again with a pleat in the centre. Tie the pudding very tightly around the rim with string and make a handle by crossing excess string across the top of the basin and tying it together. This will help you lift the pudding out of the pan once it's cooked. Trim any excess paper and foil, leaving a 2.5 cm border around the edge.

Put a heat-proof saucer or trivet in a large, deep saucepan and place the pudding basin on top. Add just enough boiled water to the pan to come halfway up the sides of the basin. Cover the pan with a tight-fitting lid and place over a low heat. Steam for 3 hours, adding more water to the pan if necessary.

For the orange brandy butter:

125 g unsalted butter, softened

75 g icing sugar

2 tablespoons Lyle's Golden Syrup

3–4 tablespoons brandy

grated zest of 1 small orange

To decorate:

small bunch of red grapes

egg white

caster sugar

holly sprig

Meanwhile, make the brandy butter: cream the butter and icing sugar together, then add the golden syrup and beat by hand or with an electric whisk until very soft. Gradually beat in the brandy and orange zest then spoon into a serving bowl. Cover and chill for at least 1 hour.

The pudding is done when a fine skewer inserted into the centre of the pudding (through the foil and paper) comes out clean. Turn off the heat and carefully lift the basin out of the water. Leave to stand for 5 minutes. The pudding can be eaten immediately, or stored for 2 weeks. To store, once cooked, re-cover with fresh parchment and foil, then keep in a cool, dark place until needed. Steam for 1 hour before serving.

To decorate:

Wash the grapes then dry them with kitchen paper. Dip in egg white then toss in caster sugar and set aside to dry. Use them to add an extra festive flourish to your pudding, along with a sprig of holly.

CRUNCHY WALNUT TART

Crumbly, crunchy, sticky, creamy and sweet: all the elements that make for a perfect tart. Use ready-made shortcrust pastry if you are short on time. Avoid using walnuts that have been hanging around in your storecupboard for months (or maybe years!), as they lose their sweetness and become quite bitter when stale.

Serves: 8

Prep: 25 minutes,
    plus chilling time
Cook: 45 minutes

For the pastry:

175 g plain flour, plus extra for dusting
pinch salt
75 g unsalted butter, chilled
    and cubed
2–3 tablespoons cold water

For the filling:

3 eggs
1 tablespoon whole milk
50 g soft dark brown sugar
175 g Lyle's Golden Syrup
50 g unsalted butter
½ teaspoon ground cinnamon
½ teaspoon vanilla extract
finely grated zest of 1 orange
175 g shelled walnut halves

To make the pastry, sift the flour and salt into a bowl then rub in the butter until the mixture resembles fine breadcrumbs. Stir in the water to bring it together into a soft but not sticky dough. Wrap the dough in clingfilm and chill for 30 minutes. Preheat the oven to 200°C/180°C fan/Gas Mark 6.

Roll out the chilled pastry on a lightly floured work surface then use it to line a 30 x 10 cm rectangular fluted flan tin. Trim off any excess pastry then line with baking parchment and cover the base with baking beans. Place the tin on a baking sheet and bake blind for 10 minutes. Remove the parchment and beans and bake for a further 5 minutes until the pastry is lightly browned. Reduce the oven temperature to 170°C/150°C fan/Gas Mark 3.

Meanwhile, make the filling. Beat the eggs and milk together in a bowl. Put the sugar and syrup in a saucepan over a low heat and warm through gently until combined. Stir in the butter, cinnamon, vanilla extract and orange zest then remove from the heat and leave to cool slightly. Slowly pour the syrup mixture into the beaten egg mixture and stir to combine.

Scatter the walnuts over the pastry case then spoon the syrup mixture over and bake for 30 minutes, or until the filling is set. Serve either hot or cold.

APPLE AND PEAR BUTTERSCOTCH PIE

This pudding pie with a sponge topping is a guaranteed crowd-pleaser: the warm fruit and butterscotch sauce sit beneath the delicious cake-like top, creating two layers. Add a little cinnamon to the filling if you fancy.

Serves: 4–6

Prep: 20 minutes
Cook: 30–35 minutes

For the filling:

2 Granny Smith apples
2 large pears, e.g. Conference
25 g unsalted butter, plus extra
    for greasing
5 tablespoons butterscotch sauce
    (shop-bought, or homemade using
    the recipe on page 27 without the
    nuts), plus extra to serve

For the topping:

115 g self-raising flour
1 teaspoon ground cinnamon
75 g unsalted butter, softened
50 g soft light brown sugar
1 large egg
50 g walnuts or pecans,
    roughly chopped
demerara sugar, for sprinkling

Preheat the oven to 180°C/160°C fan/Gas Mark 4, and grease a 1.5 litre ovenproof dish with butter.

Peel, core and thickly slice the apples and pears. Heat the butter for the filling in a large frying pan over a medium–high heat, and when melted add the fruit. Cook for 5 minutes, until the fruit is just beginning to colour. Turn out into the buttered dish and drizzle over the butterscotch sauce.

Beat together all the topping ingredients except the nuts and demerara sugar, until smooth. Drop the mixture in spoonfuls over the fruit (do not worry about the gaps as the mixture will spread during baking). Scatter the nuts and some demerara sugar over the top. Bake for 25–30 minutes, until the top is golden brown.

Remove from the oven and serve with custard or cream and extra butterscotch sauce.

picture overleaf »

GOLDEN SPONGE PUDDING

The ultimate comforting dessert for a cold winter's day. Serve warm with crème fraîche or custard (see page 128).

Serves: 6

Prep: 15 minutes

Cook: 1 ½ hours

3 rounded tablespoons Lyle's
   Golden Syrup

115 g unsalted butter, softened,
   plus extra for greasing

115 g caster sugar

2 eggs, at room temperature,
   lightly beaten

grated zest of 1 unwaxed lemon

175 g self-raising flour, sifted

1-2 tablespoons whole milk

Grease a 900 ml pudding basin with butter and pour the syrup into the bottom of the basin. Set aside.

Cream the butter and sugar together in a bowl until light and fluffy. Add the beaten eggs, a little at a time, beating well after each addition, until fully incorporated.

Add the lemon zest then, using a metal spoon, fold in the flour. Add enough milk to give the mixture a dropping consistency.

Turn the pudding mix into the prepared pudding basin and smooth the top. Pleat a circle of baking parchment and foil (cut two times larger than the diameter of the top of the pudding basin) by folding over 2.5 cm in the centre. This will allow for the pudding to expand as it cooks. Cover the basin with the parchment, with the pleat in the centre of the pudding, then cover with the foil, again with a pleat in the centre. Tie a piece of string very tightly around the rim and make a handle by crossing excess string across the top of the basin and tying it together. This will help you lift the pudding out of the pan once it's cooked. Trim any excess paper and foil, leaving a 2.5 cm border around the edge.

Put a heat-proof saucer or trivet in a large, deep saucepan and place the pudding basin on top. Add just enough boiled water to the pan to come halfway up the sides of the basin. Cover the pan with a tight-fitting lid and place the pan over a low heat. Steam for 1½ hours, adding more water to the pan if necessary.

The pudding is done when a fine skewer inserted into the centre of the pudding (through the foil and paper) comes out clean. Turn off the heat and carefully lift the basin out of the water. Leave to stand for 5 minutes.

BREAD AND BUTTER PUDDING

This much-loved traditional pud is a great treat for family meals, and what better way to use up an old loaf of bread? Leave out the booze if serving to children. Try scattering over a few chunks of dark chocolate before baking too, between the cubes of bread, to make it even more indulgent, or use brioche or fruit-studded bread in place of the white bread.

Serves: 4–6

Prep: 15 minutes, plus standing time
Cook: 30–35 minutes

300 g day-old white bread, crusts
　removed and cut into 3 cm cubes
50 g unsalted butter, plus extra for
　greasing
6 tablespoons Lyle's Golden Syrup,
　plus extra to serve
3 large eggs
150 ml double cream
450 ml whole milk
2 tablespoons rum or brandy
　(optional)
1–2 tablespoons demerara sugar,
　for sprinkling
pouring cream, to serve

Butter a 1.75 litre ovenproof dish or 4–6 individual ramekins and place the bread cubes in the dish (or divide them between the ramekins).

Place the butter and golden syrup in a saucepan and heat gently until the butter has melted, then remove from the heat and leave to cool a little.

Whisk the eggs in a bowl with the cream, milk and rum or brandy (if using), add the syrup mixture and whisk again. Pour the mixture over the bread cubes and press the bread down a little into the liquid to help it soak it up.

Leave to stand for 20 minutes. Meanwhile, preheat the oven to 180°C/160°C fan/Gas Mark 4. Place the dish or ramekins in a roasting tin and pour enough hot water to come halfway up the sides. Scatter demerara sugar over the top of the pudding(s).

Bake for 30–35 minutes (20 minutes if using ramekins), or until the top is crispy and the inside soft and slightly wobbly. Leave to stand for 10 minutes before serving with extra golden syrup and pouring cream.

FUDGE BROWNIE SUNDAE

Indulge in a bit of retro heaven with this firm favourite, which can be tweaked according to whatever you have to hand: try chocolate-flavoured ice cream, to make it super-chocolatey, or add fresh seasonal fruit.

Serves: 2

Prep: 15 minutes
Cook: 10 minutes

For the chocolate fudge sauce:

25 g dark chocolate
1 tablespoon Lyle's Golden Syrup
55 g caster sugar
3 tablespoons hot water
2 teaspoons cocoa powder
10 g cold unsalted butter
1 tablespoon cold water

To serve:

1 chocolate brownie (shop-bought,
    or Dusted Chocolate Brownies,
    see page 96)
½ x 410 g can cherries in natural juice,
    plus fresh cherries to decorate
    (optional)
2 scoops vanilla ice cream

Place the chocolate, golden syrup, caster sugar, hot water and cocoa powder in a saucepan. Warm through gently over a low heat, stirring, until the chocolate has melted and the sauce is smooth. Turn up the heat, bring to the boil and bubble for about 30 seconds, without stirring. Remove from the heat and beat in the butter and cold water. Leave to cool slightly.

Crumble the brownie, divide it between 2 sundae glasses and drizzle over a tablespoon of the cherry juice. Tumble a generous amount of cherries into each glass. Spoon half of the warm chocolate fudge sauce over the cherries, top with ice cream and the remaining sauce and decorate with a fresh cherry, if you like.

TREACLE TARTS

Enjoy these lovely treacle tarts warm or chilled, and on their own for the full golden flavour, or with a dash of crème fraîche to set off the rich depth of the golden syrup.

Makes: 4 tarts

Prep: 30 minutes, plus chilling time
Cook: 25 minutes

350 g ready-made shortcrust pastry,
   chilled
160 g Lyle's Golden Syrup
75 g fresh breadcrumbs, plus
   extra if needed
grated zest and juice of 1 lemon
1 egg white
plain flour, for dusting
butter or oil, for greasing

Grease 4 x 10 cm individual tart tins with butter and roll out three-quarters of the pastry on a lightly floured surface to around 3 mm thickness. Line the greased tart tins with the pastry and trim off any excess, ensuring you keep the trimmings. Place in the fridge for 20 minutes. Preheat the oven to 200°C/180°C fan/Gas Mark 6.

Warm the golden syrup gently in a pan until it softens. Remove the pan from the heat and stir in the breadcrumbs and the lemon zest. Set aside. Whisk the egg white in a clean, grease-free bowl until it forms stiff peaks. Fold the egg white into the breadcrumb mixture. Leave to stand for 10 minutes, then add more breadcrumbs if the mixture is too wet. Stir in 30 ml of lemon juice, then remove the lined tart tins from the fridge and spread the mixture evenly between them.

Roll out the leftover pastry on a lightly floured surface and cut it into 28 thin strips. Don't worry about being too precise. Arrange the strips, straight or twisted, in lattice form over each tart (or just a couple of tarts if you'd like to keep some plain).

Bake the tarts for 10 minutes, then reduce the oven temperature to 190°C/170°C fan/Gas Mark 5 and bake for a further 15 minutes until golden. Remove from the oven and leave to cool in the tins before carefully turning out to serve.

KNICKERBOCKER GLORY

You can go as crazy as you like with the flavour combinations in this retro dessert – just don't forget the syrup! Try adding vanilla seeds scraped from half a vanilla pod to the cream, before you whisk it, and use any flavour of ice cream you fancy. Mango or raspberries work well in place of the strawberries too, if you prefer.

Serves: 4

Prep: 15 minutes, plus setting time

135 g packet strawberry-flavoured jelly
150 ml double cream
2 muffins or small sponges, cut into small pieces
400 g fresh strawberries, hulled and halved
Lyle's Golden Syrup, for drizzling
vanilla ice cream
toasted flaked almonds
4 ice cream wafer fans

Make the jelly by following the packet instructions, then pour it into a shallow baking dish and chill for 2 hours, or until set. Once the jelly is set, cut it into approximately 1.5 cm cubes then turn the cubes out of the dish into a bowl.

Whisk the cream in a separate bowl until it forms soft peaks.

Take 4 tall sundae glasses and place a layer of muffin or cake pieces in the bottom of each one. Add a layer of halved strawberries. Drizzle over some golden syrup (to taste) and add a small scoop of ice cream to each glass.

Add a layer of jelly pieces to each glass, then more golden syrup, followed by another layer of strawberries and ice cream. Top each glass with a swirl of whipped cream. Decorate with flaked almonds, strawberries and more syrup, and finish with an ice cream wafer fan. Serve immediately with a long spoon.

HOT FRUIT SALAD

This pud might be sweet, but it's also jam-packed with vitamin C. Try swapping the fruit for whatever fruit you have to hand, perhaps fresh peaches or apricots. Ring the changes with the spices, too – a pinch of mixed spice in place of the cinnamon and cloves works a treat.

Serves: 6

Prep: 10 minutes
Cook: 30–40 minutes

butter, for greasing
2 nectarines
4 plums
1 small fresh pineapple
2 tablespoons Lyle's Golden Syrup
150 ml apple juice
1 cinnamon stick
3 whole cloves
mascarpone cheese or crème fraîche,
   to serve

Preheat the oven to 180°C/160°C fan/Gas Mark 4 and grease a large, shallow ovenproof dish with butter. Cut around the nectarines and plums, following the natural line, then twist the halves in opposite directions to separate. Remove the stones and cut each of the nectarine halves in half again. Arrange the nectarines and plums in a single layer in the baking dish.

Prepare the pineapple: cut away and discard the outer skin and tough fibrous core. Cut the pineapple flesh into generously sized chunks and add to the fruit in the dish.

Drizzle the golden syrup over all the fruits, then pour in the apple juice. Tuck in the cinnamon stick and cloves. Bake, uncovered, in the oven for 30–40 minutes, basting the fruit with the juice a couple of times during cooking, until the fruits are tender.

Remove from the oven and discard the cinnamon stick and cloves. Serve warm with a big dollop of mascarpone cheese or crème fraîche.

NUTTY BUTTERSCOTCH ICE CREAM

Making ice cream at home can be a time-consuming venture, but this rich, smooth ice cream is quick and simple (you don't need to make a custard base), and utterly delicious.

Serves: 4–6

Prep: 5 minutes, plus churning/
freezing and softening time

500 g natural Greek yoghurt

150 ml double cream

6 tablespoons Nutty Butterscotch
Sauce (see page 27) or shop-
bought sauce, plus extra to serve

50 g pecans, chopped, plus extra
to serve

Tip the yoghurt into a bowl, add the cream and the butterscotch sauce and stir to mix. Freeze the mixture in an ice-cream maker according to the manufacturer's instructions, adding the chopped nuts when the mixture is beginning to thicken. Turn out into a freezer-proof container and freeze if not serving immediately. Alternatively, if you don't have an ice-cream maker, pour the mixture into a freezer-proof container and freeze, uncovered, until thick, then scrape the sides of the mixture into the centre with a fork or spoon and stir, then cover and return to the freezer. Repeat until the ice cream is smooth and fully frozen.

Before serving, transfer the ice cream to the fridge for 30 minutes to soften a little before scooping into glasses, and serve with extra butterscotch sauce for pouring, and extra chopped nuts.

Lyle's Tips

You could use salted peanuts instead of the pecans.

Sandwich the ice cream between chocolate cookies, along with a drizzle of syrup, to make an ice cream sandwich.

RHUBARB AND APPLE SYRUP OAT CRUMBLE

The tang of rhubarb works beautifully with the light crunch of the oaty crumble in this classic pud, which can be made in individual ramekin dishes or one large dish. Perfect served with warm custard (see page 128) or a drizzle of double cream.

Serves: 6–8

Prep: 20 minutes

Cook: 35–40 minutes

500 g rhubarb, trimmed and cut into 3 cm lengths

500 g Bramley apples, peeled, cored and diced

1 teaspoon plain flour

3 tablespoons Lyle's Golden Syrup

For the crumble topping:

75 g chilled unsalted butter, cubed, plus extra for greasing

75 g plain flour

115 g rolled porridge oats

50 g demerara sugar

½ teaspoon ground cinnamon

Preheat the oven to 180°C/160°C fan/Gas Mark 4 and lightly grease an ovenproof dish with butter.

Place the fruit in the dish, add the flour, toss to distribute the flour evenly among the pieces of fruit, then drizzle over the golden syrup.

To make the crumble topping, put the butter in a large bowl with the flour and oats. Gently rub the butter into the mixture with your fingertips until the mixture resembles breadcrumbs, then add the sugar and cinnamon and mix to combine.

Scatter the crumble mix in an even layer over the fruit and bake for 35–40 minutes, until golden brown. Remove from the oven and serve.

Lyle's Tips

If you have time, pop the crumble mixture in the freezer for a few minutes. It will make the topping extra crumbly when baked.

Try crushing a handful of amaretti biscuits and adding them to the crumble mixture, to give a rich almond flavour.

CHOCOLATE CHESTNUT POTS

An effortless, do-ahead recipe, these divine and softly set chocolate pots have a fabulous smooth texture, with amaretti biscuits adding a lovely light, crunchy finish.

Serves: 6

Prep: 25 minutes
Cook: 5 minutes, plus setting time

For the pots:

200 g dark chocolate (minimum 70 per cent cocoa solids), broken into squares
120 ml double cream
120 ml whole milk
225 g unsweetened chestnut purée
1 large egg
60 g Lyle's Golden Syrup
1 tablespoon coffee liqueur or brandy
75 g soft amaretti biscuits, broken into chunks

To serve:

2 rounded tablespoons unsweetened chestnut purée
40 g Lyle's Golden Syrup, plus extra for drizzling
120 ml double cream
3 marrons glacés, halved

Place the chocolate, cream and milk in a small non-stick saucepan over a low heat for 4–5 minutes until the chocolate has melted, then whisk until smooth. Remove from the heat and set aside.

Put the chestnut purée in the bowl of a food processor and blend until smooth. Pour the warm chocolate mixture into the bowl, then add the egg, golden syrup, coffee liqueur or brandy and blend again. Scrape down the mixture from the sides of the bowl. Add the amaretti biscuits and pulse briefly, just long enough to combine.

Divide the mixture between 6 small pots, cover with clingfilm and chill for 3–4 hours until set.

When you're ready to serve, mash the 2 rounded tablespoons of chestnut purée in a small bowl with the back of a teaspoon until fairly smooth, then stir in the golden syrup. Whisk the cream in a bowl until it forms soft peaks then stir in the chestnut purée mixture, folding it through to marble the cream (don't fully incorporate it). Divide the cream between the chocolate pots, arrange the marrons glacés halves on top, then drizzle over a little golden syrup and serve.

QUICK GLAZED STRAWBERRY TARTS

Luscious red strawberry tarts are a must every summer. This is a simply perfect strawberry tart recipe that brings out the very best in our favourite berry.

Serves: 4

Prep: 10 minutes
Cook: 10–15 minutes

1 x 215 g sheet, ready-rolled
   all-butter puff pastry
2 tablespoons whole milk, for glazing
200 ml double cream
1 tablespoon Lyle's Golden Syrup,
   plus extra for glazing
225 g fresh strawberries, hulled
   and quartered

Preheat the oven to 190°C/170°C fan/Gas Mark 5 and line a baking tray with baking parchment.

Lay out the puff pastry and, with a 10 cm pastry cutter or an upside-down glass, cut out 4 rounds. With a smaller 7.5 cm pastry cutter (or a smaller upside-down glass), score a smaller circle within the larger disc, but not all the way through. Glaze the pastry with the milk.

Carefully lay the pastry discs, with the middle and outer edge intact, on the lined tray and bake for 10 minutes, or until risen, crisp and golden. Remove from the oven and leave to cool on a wire rack.

Whisk the double cream in a bowl until it forms soft peaks.

Very carefully cut around the inner circle (that was scored with the smaller pastry cutter) of each pastry disc with a small, sharp knife and remove the excess pastry from the middle to leave a crisp pastry case.

Mix the golden syrup into the whipped cream to make a delicate, sweet Chantilly cream. Fill the cases with the cream and top with mounds of strawberries. Heat through a little more golden syrup and use a pastry brush to glaze the strawberries before serving.

Lyle's Tip

Try making quick glazed plum tarts: spread the golden syrup over the unbaked pastry discs, top each with half a plum, cut side down, brush with melted butter, sprinkle with a little sugar and ground cinnamon and bake for 12 minutes. Serve with the Chantilly cream above.

CUSTARD

A classic comforting custard, given a welcome syrupy edge, that is the perfect accompaniment for Golden Sponge Pudding (see page 114), Rhubarb and Apple Syrup Oat Crumble (see page 124) and Apple and Pear Butterscotch Pie (see page 111). Serve it piping hot.

Serves: 2

Prep: 25 minutes

300 ml single cream

250 ml whole milk

3 egg yolks

80 g Lyle's Golden Syrup, plus extra for drizzling

Combine the single cream and whole milk in a small saucepan over a medium heat, and bring to just a touch under the boil. Remove from the heat.

Whisk the egg yolks and golden syrup together in a bowl until pale and frothy. Gradually whisk the yolk and syrup mixture into the hot milk mixture.

Transfer to a clean saucepan and whisk continuously over a low heat for 10–15 minutes, or until the custard thickens enough to coat the back of a wooden spoon. Do not overheat. If you feel nervous about cooking the custard over a direct heat, make it in a heat-proof bowl over a pan of simmering water instead, but make sure the bottom of the bowl isn't touching the water (it may take a little longer to thicken).

Remove from the heat and strain the custard through a sieve into a clean jug or bowl. Drizzle a little golden syrup into the custard before serving.

Lyle's Tip

To make a vanilla custard, add the scraped seeds of a vanilla pod to the cream and milk in step 1.

CREAM CRANACHAN

This classic Scottish dessert with golden toasted oatmeal is hard to beat. You could use toasted porridge oats instead of oatmeal, or take a shortcut and use granola!

Serves: 4

Prep: 25 minutes, plus chilling time

50 g medium oatmeal
300 ml double cream
4 tablespoons Lyle's Golden Syrup
3 tablespoons whisky
350 g fresh raspberries

Toast the oatmeal in a grill pan (without the rack) or dry non-stick frying pan until golden brown, stirring occasionally. Set aside and leave for about 15 minutes to cool.

Whisk the cream in a bowl until it forms soft peaks, then fold in the golden syrup, whisky and cooled toasted oatmeal. Reserve a few raspberries for decoration, then layer the remaining raspberries and cream mixture in 4 glasses.

Cover the glasses with clingfilm and chill for about 1 hour before serving, decorated with the reserved raspberries.

CARAMELISED CARIBBEAN PINEAPPLE

If you want to cook this sticky tropical treat on the barbecue, thread the pineapple wedges onto metal or soaked wooden skewers beforehand, and if you're making it for kids, leave out the rum and add a squeeze of lime juice to the sauce instead, to give it a citrus tang.

Serves: 4

Prep: 5 minutes
Cook: 6–10 minutes

1 ripe pineapple, cored and cut
 lengthways into 8 wedges
100 ml dark rum
1 cinnamon stick
1 teaspoon vanilla extract
2 tablespoons water
50 g soft light brown sugar
100 g Lyle's Golden Syrup
vanilla ice cream, to serve (optional)

Heat a griddle pan or barbecue grill until hot, pat the pineapple wedges dry with kitchen paper then lay them on the griddle or barbecue grill and cook for 3 minutes, until char marks appear, then flip them over and cook for a further 3 minutes. Remove and place on warm plates.

While the pineapple wedges are cooking, make the sauce. Put the rum, cinnamon stick, vanilla extract and water in a small saucepan, add the sugar and stir to dissolve. Bring to the boil then cook for a few minutes. Pour in the syrup and cook for a further 3 minutes, stirring frequently, until the sauce has thickened slightly. Serve the pineapple with the sauce poured over and scoops of vanilla ice cream, if you like.

RICH CHOCOLATE MOUSSE

Serve this beautifully rich chocolate mousse in small glasses, and sprinkle with the popping candy (just at the last minute or it will lose its 'pop') or amaretti biscuits if you like. Delicious served with physalis to cut through the richness. You can make the mousse up to 2 days ahead and store, covered, in the fridge.

Serves: 6

Prep: 20 minutes
Cook: 5 minutes, plus chilling time

150 g dark chocolate (minimum 70 per cent cocoa solids), broken into squares

4 large eggs, at room temperature, separated

25 g Lyle's Golden Syrup

25 g golden caster sugar

2 tablespoons brandy (optional)

1 tablespoon cocoa powder, sifted

150 ml double cream

2 rounded tablespoons popping candy, 6 physalis or 6 amaretti biscuits (optional)

Put the chocolate in a small heat-proof bowl and set it over a small saucepan of simmering water, making sure the bowl doesn't touch the water, and stir until melted – about 5 minutes – or microwave for about 1 minute, in 20-second bursts. Remove from the heat and set aside.

Combine the egg yolks, golden syrup and golden caster sugar in a mixing bowl and beat well with an electric hand mixer for about 3 minutes, until thickened. Mix in the brandy, if using, and cocoa powder.

Lightly whisk the double cream until slightly thickened and it just holds its shape. Fold the whipped cream into the egg and sugar mixture, then fold in the melted chocolate until it is fully incorporated.

Finally, whisk the egg whites in a clean, grease-free bowl until they form soft peaks then lightly fold them into the chocolate mixture with a large metal spoon. Divide between 6 glasses or small serving dishes and chill for 1–2 hours, or until softly set. If you're chilling the mousse in advance or overnight, let it soften slightly for 5–10 minutes at room temperature before serving.

Top with popping candy or crumbled amaretti biscuits, and decorate with physalis, if you like.

RASPBERRY YOGHURT ICE

Try replacing raspberries in this refreshing summer dessert with other seasonal fruits such as strawberries, blackberries, blueberries and blackcurrants (using a little more icing sugar to sweeten, if necessary). Use pasteurised egg white if you are worried about serving raw egg.

Serves: 6

Prep: 20 minutes, plus freezing and softening time

400 g fresh or thawed frozen
   raspberries
40–50 g icing sugar, sifted
2 tablespoons Lyle's Golden Syrup
300 ml natural Greek yoghurt
2 egg whites, at room temperature
150 ml extra thick double cream
fresh raspberries and mint leaves,
   to serve

Push the raspberries through a fine-mesh sieve with a wooden spoon over a mixing bowl to catch all the juices. Discard the seeds. Stir half the icing sugar and all the golden syrup into the raspberry purée then add the yoghurt and whisk until completely smooth.

Whisk the egg whites in a clean, grease-free bowl until stiff then fold in the remaining icing sugar. To test if the egg whites are stiff enough, slowly turn the bowl upside down and the whites should remain in the bowl. Fold the whisked egg whites and double cream into the raspberry mixture.

Pour the mixture into a freezer-proof container. Cover with a lid and freeze for 2–3 hours, or until ice crystals have formed. Remove from the freezer and beat well with a fork or small whisk to break down the ice crystals. Re-freeze until solid.

Remove from the freezer 30 minutes before required and serve in scoops with fresh raspberries and mint leaves.

CAKES AND TEATIME TREATS

VICTORIA SPONGE

A baking classic, with a golden syrup twist. Our take on the Victoria sandwich puts a smile on your face – and a warm feeling in your tummy. Wheel it out for afternoon tea, or serve it to top off a memorable meal... it's the perfect dessert.

Serves: 6–8

Prep: 30 minutes
Cook: 30–35 minutes,
    plus cooling time

For the cake:

275 g unsalted butter, softened,
    plus extra for greasing
150 g Lyle's Golden Syrup
125 g golden caster sugar
5 large eggs, at room temperature,
    lightly beaten
275 g self-raising flour
1 rounded teaspoon baking powder
1 tablespoon whole milk

For the filling and decoration:

175 ml double cream, lightly whipped
5 rounded tablespoons raspberry jam
icing sugar, to dust

Preheat the oven to 170°C/150°C fan/Gas Mark 3. Grease two 20 cm round sandwich tins and line them with greaseproof paper.

Place the butter, golden syrup and sugar in a bowl and beat by hand or with an electric hand mixer until light and creamy.

Add the eggs a little at a time, beating well after each addition. It doesn't matter if the mixture curdles as it will come together once you add the flour.

Sift the flour and baking powder into the egg and butter mixture then lightly and quickly fold it in with a large metal spoon. Add the milk to give the batter a soft consistency (so it drops easily from the spoon).

Divide the mixture between the prepared tins, level the surface and bake for 30–35 minutes until golden brown, well risen and the cakes spring back when lightly pressed with a finger. A fine skewer inserted into the middle of each cake should come out clean. Remove from the oven and leave the cakes to cool for 20 minutes in their tins, then turn out onto a wire rack to cool, removing the greaseproof paper.

Whisk the double cream for the filling in a bowl until it forms soft peaks. Sandwich the cooled cakes together with the jam and whipped cream then dust with a little icing sugar and you're ready to serve. Your only challenge now? Eat without getting icing on your nose...

COFFEE AND WALNUT CAKE

Trust golden syrup to add even more class to this classic confection.
Perfect for elevenses (or any time).

Serves: 12

Prep: 1 hour
Cook: 30–35 minutes,
    plus cooling time

For the cake:

350 g unsalted butter, softened, plus
    extra for greasing
350 g Lyle's Golden Syrup
2 rounded tablespoons instant
    espresso powder
6 large eggs, at room temperature,
    lightly beaten
110 g ground almonds
250 g self-raising flour, sifted
110 g walnuts, roughly chopped

For the caramelised walnuts:

110 g Lyle's Golden Syrup
12 walnut halves

For the buttercream:

225 g unsalted butter, softened
225 g icing sugar
165 g Lyle's Golden Syrup
3 rounded tablespoons instant
    espresso powder

Preheat the oven to 170°C/150°C fan/Gas Mark 3. Grease two 20 cm round sandwich tins and line with greaseproof paper.

Place the butter and golden syrup in a bowl and beat by hand or with an electric hand mixer until light and creamy, then mix in the espresso powder. Add the eggs a little at a time, beating well after each addition. Combine the almonds and flour and carefully fold them into the mixture, then add the chopped walnuts.

Divide the mixture between the two prepared tins, level the surface and bake for 30–35 minutes, until risen and golden brown. A fine skewer inserted into the middle of each cake should come out clean. Remove from the oven and leave the cakes to cool for 10 minutes in their tins, then turn out onto a wire rack to cool, removing the greaseproof paper.

To make the caramelised walnuts, heat the golden syrup in a frying pan for 3–4 minutes until bubbling and a rich caramel colour (don't stir; just shake the pan occasionally). Line two baking trays with baking parchment. Check the golden syrup caramel is ready by dropping a little of it into a bowl of ice-cold water – if it hardens immediately, remove from the heat. If not, heat for another minute then test again. Add the walnuts to the caramel and swirl them with a fork, to coat. Tip onto one of the lined baking trays, then drizzle any remaining caramel onto the other tray in a pattern, to make 12 decorative pieces. Leave to cool and harden.

To make the buttercream, place the butter in a bowl and sift over the icing sugar. Add the golden syrup and beat for 1 minute (by hand or with an electric hand mixer) until soft. Dissolve the espresso powder in 2 tablespoons of boiling water, add to the buttercream mixture and combine until smooth.

Sandwich the cooled cakes together with half of the buttercream and spread the rest over the top. Place on a serving plate, decorate with the caramelised walnuts and caramel pieces and serve.

BABYCHINO CUPCAKES

Delicious served as a cake, or as a dessert with a glass of coffee liqueur. You can serve the cupcakes just in their paper cases, but we think they're extra special served in coffee cups with the whipped cream topping resembling frothy milk.

Makes: 12 cupcakes

Prep: 40 minutes
Cook: 18–20 minutes,
    plus cooling time

For the cupcakes:

3 tablespoons whole milk

2 level teaspoons instant
    coffee powder

110 g unsalted butter, cubed, softened

25 g Lyle's Golden Syrup

125 g soft light brown sugar

125 g self-raising flour

25 g cocoa powder, plus extra to dust

2 large eggs

For the coffee syrup and topping:

3 level teaspoons instant
    coffee powder

2 tablespoons boiling water

4 tablespoons Lyle's Golden Syrup

310 ml double cream

Preheat the oven to 180°C/160°C fan/Gas Mark 4 and line a 12-hole muffin tin with paper cases. Heat the milk until boiling and stir in the coffee until dissolved.

Place the butter, golden syrup, soft light brown sugar, self-raising flour, cocoa powder and eggs in a bowl with the coffee mixture. Beat together with an electric hand mixer for about 1 minute, until soft and creamy.

Divide the mixture between the paper cases and bake on the middle shelf of the oven for 18–20 minutes, until well risen and the cakes spring back when lightly pressed with a finger.

Meanwhile, for the coffee syrup, dissolve the coffee powder in the boiling water then stir in the golden syrup.

Transfer the cupcakes to a wire rack to cool. Peel off the paper cases, lightly poke them all over with a fine skewer, then push the cakes down a little into 12 small coffee cups. Drizzle over the coffee syrup and leave to soak in for a few minutes.

Lightly whisk the double cream in a bowl until it forms soft peaks. Spoon the whipped cream onto the cakes and, using a small palette knife, spread it gently to the edges of the cups, and into a swirl in the middle. Dust with cocoa powder, place on saucers or a tray and serve.

STICKY GINGER FAIRY CAKES

Moist and subtly spiced with warming ginger, these fairy cakes are teatime perfection. If you love ginger as much as we do, you might like to add some finely chopped crystallised stem ginger to the cake mix or use it to decorate the iced cakes.

Makes: 12 fairy cakes

Prep: 15 minutes
Cook: 30 minutes,
   plus cooling time

150 g soft dark brown sugar
115 g Lyle's Golden Syrup
75 g Lyle's Black Treacle
175 g unsalted butter
225 g plain flour
½ teaspoon bicarbonate of soda
1 tablespoon ground ginger
½ teaspoon ground cinnamon
2 eggs, lightly beaten
150 ml whole milk

For the icing:

175 g icing sugar
juice of 1 lemon

Preheat the oven to 180°C/160°C fan/Gas Mark 4 and line a 12-hole muffin tin with paper cases.

Put the soft dark brown sugar in a saucepan with the golden syrup, black treacle and butter, place over a medium heat and stir until the butter has melted. Remove from the heat.

Sift the flour into a bowl with the bicarbonate of soda and spices, add the eggs, milk and melted mixture. Quickly combine, then spoon the mixture into the paper cases (you might find it easier to pour the mixture into the cases from a jug).

Bake for 30 minutes, remove from the oven and leave to cool for 5 minutes before lifting the cakes out of the tin and transferring them to a wire rack to cool completely.

For the icing, sift the icing sugar into a bowl, add enough lemon juice to make a thick dripping consistency, then spoon or drizzle the icing onto the cakes. Leave to set.

ROCKY ROAD CUPCAKES

This one-bowl cake mix couldn't be simpler or quicker. And it's great to get kids involved in the rocky-road-style decoration!

Makes: 12 cupcakes

Prep: 45 minutes
Cook: 20–25 minutes,
   plus cooling time

For the cupcakes:

175 g unsalted butter, softened
150 g soft light brown sugar
25 g Lyle's Golden Syrup
3 large eggs, at room temperature
175 g self-raising flour
20 g cocoa powder
1 rounded teaspoon baking powder
110 g dark chocolate (minimum
   70 per cent cocoa solids), broken
   into small pieces

For the buttercream:

60 g unsalted butter, softened
2 tablespoons Lyle's Golden Syrup
95 g icing sugar
25 g cocoa powder

To decorate:

265 g mini chocolate Easter eggs
40 g mini marshmallows
25 g flaked almonds
cocoa powder, for dusting

Preheat the oven to 180°C/160°C fan/Gas Mark 4 and line a 12-hole muffin tin with paper cases.

Place the butter, soft light brown sugar, golden syrup and eggs together in a bowl, then sift over the flour, cocoa powder and baking powder. Beat together with an electric hand mixer for about 1 minute, until soft and creamy, then fold in the pieces of chocolate.

Divide the mixture evenly between the paper cases and bake for 20–25 minutes until well risen and the cakes spring back when lightly pressed with a finger. Remove from the oven and transfer the cupcakes to a wire rack to cool.

To make the buttercream, beat together the butter and golden syrup in a mixing bowl. Sift over the icing sugar and cocoa powder and beat with a wooden spoon until smooth and creamy.

Spoon the buttercream onto the cupcakes and, using a small palette knife, lightly spread it to the edges of the cases. Arrange the Easter eggs, marshmallows and almonds on top, slightly pressing them into the buttercream. Spoon a little cocoa powder into a small sieve and lightly dust the cakes. Arrange on a plate and serve.

CARROT CAKE

Gently spiced, beautifully light and brought to life with the magic of golden syrup.

Serves: 12

Prep: 30 minutes
Cook: 1 hour,
    plus cooling time

unsalted butter, for greasing
80 g soft light brown sugar
185 ml sunflower oil
125 g Lyle's Golden Syrup, plus
    extra for drizzling
3 eggs, at room temperature
1 teaspoon vanilla extract
150 g self-raising flour
75 g plain flour
1 teaspoon bicarbonate of soda
½ teaspoon ground cinnamon
pinch freshly grated nutmeg
2 large carrots, peeled and grated

For the icing:

150 g full-fat cream cheese
80 g icing sugar
½ teaspoon vanilla extract

Preheat the oven to 170°C/150°C fan/Gas Mark 3. Grease a 23 cm loaf tin with butter and line it with greaseproof paper or baking parchment.

Combine the brown sugar, sunflower oil, golden syrup, eggs and vanilla extract in a large bowl and whisk until well combined.

Sift the flours, bicarbonate of soda, cinnamon and nutmeg over the syrup mixture and use a wooden spoon to gently combine. Stir in the grated carrots.

Pour the cake mixture into the prepared tin and bake for 1 hour, or until golden brown and well risen. A fine skewer inserted into the middle of the cake should come out clean. Remove from the oven and leave the cake to cool for 10 minutes in its tin, then turn it out onto a wire rack to cool, removing the greaseproof paper or parchment.

To make the icing, place the cream cheese, icing sugar and vanilla extract in a bowl and beat together with a wooden spoon.

Spread the icing over the cooled cake then serve, or store in an airtight tin for up to 1 week.

GOLDEN SYRUP CUPCAKES

Delicious cupcakes, with that baked-in Lyle's warming taste. Make with luscious buttercream for the full effect, or simply enjoy them on their own.

Makes: 12 cupcakes

Prep: 25 minutes
Cook: 20–25 minutes,
     plus cooling time

For the cupcakes:

185 g unsalted butter, softened
3 tablespoons Lyle's Golden Syrup
150 g golden caster sugar
185 g self-raising flour
3 large eggs
2 tablespoons whole milk

For the buttercream and decoration:

110 g unsalted butter, softened
200 g icing sugar, plus extra for
     dusting
2 tablespoons Lyle's Golden Syrup,
     plus extra for drizzling
1 tablespoon whole milk

Preheat the oven to 180°C/160°C fan/Gas Mark 4 and line a 12-hole muffin tin with paper cases.

Place the butter, golden syrup, golden caster sugar, self-raising flour, eggs and milk in a bowl. Beat with an electric hand mixer for about 1 minute, until soft and creamy.

Divide the mixture between the paper cases and bake on the middle shelf of the oven for 20–25 minutes, until well risen, golden brown and the cakes spring back when lightly pressed with a finger. Remove from the oven and transfer the cupcakes to a wire rack to cool.

For the buttercream, put the butter in a bowl, sift over the icing sugar and mix until soft, then add the golden syrup and milk and stir until smooth. Transfer to a piping bag fitted with a star nozzle and decorate the cakes with swirls of buttercream. Drizzle over a little golden syrup, lightly dust with icing sugar and serve.

Lyle's Tip

If you prefer chocolate icing, melt 100 g dark chocolate, then remove from the heat and add a tablespoon of golden syrup and 25 g unsalted butter. Stir until the mixture reaches the right consistency, then transfer to a piping bag and decorate the cakes as above.

CHOCOLATEY FUDGE CAKE

Moist and light, everyone will love this perfect, luscious and rich chocolate cake.

Serves: 8–10

Prep: 30 minutes
Cook: 30 minutes,
    plus cooling time

For the cake:

75 g cocoa powder
160 ml boiling water
150 g unsalted butter, softened,
    plus extra for greasing
110 g Lyle's Golden Syrup
315 g golden caster sugar
4 large eggs
75 ml whole milk
250 g plain flour
1½ rounded teaspoons baking powder

For the filling, icing and decoration:

150 g dark chocolate (70 per cent
    cocoa solids), broken into pieces
150 ml double cream
1 tablespoon Lyle's Golden Syrup

Preheat the oven to 180°C/160°C fan/Gas Mark 4 and grease two 20 cm deep sandwich tins with butter, then line the bases with baking parchment or greaseproof paper.

In a large bowl mix the cocoa powder and water with a wooden spoon until smooth, then add the butter, golden syrup, caster sugar, eggs and milk. Mix again, until thoroughly incorporated, then sift over the flour and baking powder and fold in to make a thick batter.

Spoon the mixture into the prepared tins and bake on the middle shelf of the oven for 30 minutes, or until risen and a fine skewer comes out clean when inserted into the centre of the cakes. Leave to cool for 10 minutes, then turn out onto a wire rack and remove the greaseproof paper or baking parchment.

For the filling and icing, combine the chocolate, cream and golden syrup in a heat-proof bowl and set the bowl over a pan of simmering water, stirring constantly, until the chocolate has melted (make sure that the bowl isn't touching the water). Remove from the heat and leave to cool and thicken to a spreading consistency.

Sandwich the two cakes together with about half of the chocolate cream, arrange on a plate, then use a palette knife to spread the rest of the icing over the top.

SWISH SWISS ROLL

Roll up for this special treat. Quick and easy to make, this cracking Swiss roll is light and airy — but still has that unmistakeable intensity of golden syrup.

Serves: 8

Prep: 20 minutes
Cook: 10–12 minutes

unsalted butter, for greasing
3 large eggs, at room temperature
75 g Lyle's Golden Syrup, plus
   1 tablespoon for the cream
75 g self-raising flour
golden caster sugar, for sprinkling
6 rounded tablespoons raspberry jam
120 ml double cream

Lyle's Tip

Longing for a chocolate version? Just swap 25 g (a heaped tablespoon) of cocoa powder for one of flour, then fill the roll with a rich chocolate buttercream.

Preheat the oven to 200°C/180°C fan/Gas Mark 6. Grease a 23 x 30 cm Swiss roll tin with butter and line it with baking parchment.

Whisk the eggs and golden syrup in a bowl until thick, pale and fluffy.

Sift over the flour and lightly fold it in, then spoon the mixture into the prepared tin, spreading it carefully to the edges.

Bake for 10–12 minutes, until golden brown, light and springy. While the sponge is baking, place a sheet of baking parchment at least as big as the Swiss roll tin on a work surface and sprinkle it with golden caster sugar.

Remove the sponge from the oven and immediately turn it out onto the sugar-sprinkled baking parchment. Carefully peel away the baking parchment attached to the sponge from baking, and trim all the edges with a sharp knife. Score a line along the length of the sponge nearest you, about 2.5 cm in from the edge – don't cut all the way through. This will help you make a nice, tight roll.

Leave to cool for about 10 minutes. While it's cooling, warm the jam gently until it's runny (on the hob or in the microwave). Spread the jam all over the cooled sponge, right to the edges.

Lightly whisk the cream with the remaining 1 tablespoon of golden syrup until it forms soft peaks. Spread on top of the jam, but not quite to the edges.

Starting with the scored edge closest to you, use the paper under the sponge to roll the cake away from you, tightly rolling it up as you do. Carefully transfer to a serving dish with the seam on the underside and sprinkle with a little more golden caster sugar. Slice to serve.

LEMON SYRUP CAKE

This lemon drizzle cake – a teatime favourite – drizzled with warm golden syrup, is given extra tangy oomph with a lemon icing.

Serves: 8

Prep: 25 minutes
Cook: 45–50 minutes,
    plus cooling time

200 g unsalted butter, softened,
    plus extra for greasing
200 g caster sugar
grated zest and juice of 1 large
    unwaxed lemon
3 eggs, beaten
200 g self-raising flour
75 g sultanas
3 rounded tablespoons Lyle's
    Golden Syrup

For the icing:

175 g full-fat cream cheese
40 g unsalted butter, softened
grated zest of ½ unwaxed lemon
50 g icing sugar

Grease a 20 cm round, deep springform cake tin with butter and line with greaseproof paper. Preheat the oven to 180°C/160°C fan/ Gas Mark 4.

Place the butter, sugar and lemon zest in a bowl and beat by hand or with an electric hand mixer until light and fluffy.

Add the eggs a little at a time, beating well after each addition. It doesn't matter if the mixture curdles as it will come together once you add the flour. Sift the flour over the mixture, then add the sultanas. Fold together to combine.

Pour the mixture into the prepared tin, then level the surface and bake for 45–50 minutes, or until the cake springs back when lightly touched. A fine skewer inserted into the middle of the cake should come out clean. Remove from the oven and set aside (with the cake still in its tin).

Warm the golden syrup and the lemon juice in a saucepan and slowly spoon it over the hot cake. Leave to cool in the tin before turning out.

To make the icing, place the cream cheese, butter, lemon zest and icing sugar in a bowl and beat together until soft and smooth. Spread the icing evenly over the top of the cake.

Lyle's Tip

For extra decoration, add small blobs of lemon curd onto the icing and swirl with the tip of a knife.

CLASSIC CHRISTMAS CAKE

Special occasions deserve special cakes. This rich, luxuriant bake is perfect for your memorable Christmas dinner. You can also use this recipe for a wedding or christening cake.

Serves: 12–16

Prep: 1½ hours, plus drying time
Cook: 3½ hours, plus cooling time

For the cake:

210 ml whisky or brandy

grated zest and juice of 1 orange

3 teaspoons vanilla extract

125 g Lyle's Golden Syrup, plus
   1 tablespoon

2 level teaspoons mixed spice

450 g raisins

225 g dried cranberries

110 g pitted prunes, roughly chopped

50 g glacé cherries, halved, rinsed,
   dried and finely chopped

110 g candied peel, chopped

50 g blanched almonds, roughly
   chopped

250 g unsalted butter, at room
   temperature, plus extra for greasing

125 g dark muscovado sugar

250 g self-raising flour

5 large eggs, at room temperature,
   lightly beaten

½ level teaspoon salt

225 ml whisky or brandy, for feeding
   the cake (optional)

Grease a 20 cm round cake tin with butter and line the base and sides with a double layer of baking parchment.

Place the whisky or brandy, orange juice and zest, vanilla extract, the 1 tablespoon of golden syrup and the mixed spice in a large saucepan. Add the raisins, cranberries, prunes, glacé cherries, candied peel and almonds. Stir, bring to just under the boil, then turn down to a simmer for 5 minutes. Stir once or twice, until the liquid has been absorbed and the fruit has plumped up nicely. Remove from the heat and leave to cool.

Preheat the oven to 140°C/120°C fan/Gas Mark 1 with the shelf set on the middle. Place the butter, golden syrup and dark muscovado sugar in a large mixing bowl, beat until soft and fluffy, then add the flour, eggs and salt. Mix well until smooth, then stir in the cooled fruit mixture until well combined.

Spoon the cake mixture into the prepared tin. Level the surface and make a gentle hollow in the middle (you don't want the cake to peak too much). Bake for 3 hours, then cover the surface of the cake with a double layer of baking parchment. Bake the cake for a further 20–30 minutes, or until the centre springs back nicely when lightly touched.

Leave the cake to cool in the tin for 30 minutes then turn out onto a wire rack to finish cooling. Peel off the parchment. If you like, feed the cake with whisky or brandy at intervals over a month to enrich it: poke holes in the cake with a fine skewer or cocktail stick then drip about 2 tablespoons of the alcohol over the top each time. Wrap in foil between feeds and store in an airtight container – it will keep for up to 3 months.

continued »

For the decoration:

3 rounded tablespoons smooth
  apricot jam

1 tablespoon water

500 g white marzipan

icing sugar, for dusting

500 g white fondant icing

light green and dark green fondant
  icing colour

edible cake glue or icing sugar
  mixed with water

edible gold cake pearls

ribbon, for cake trim

Transfer the cake to a 25.5 cm round cake board. Heat the jam and water in a small saucepan for 2–3 minutes, stir to combine, then brush all over the cake.

Roll out the marzipan on a surface dusted with icing sugar to a circle shape large enough to cover the cake. Roll the marzipan carefully around the rolling pin then unroll it onto the cake. Cut away the excess and leave out to dry. The next day, repeat using the fondant icing.

Divide the fondant trimmings (you should have about 95 g left over) in two and add the fondant colour – one light green, one dark green – kneading the colour into the icing until it's evenly distributed. Re-roll each colour and stamp out 18 holly leaves (9 of each colour) with a holly leaf cutter. Use edible cake glue to stick them on top of the cake. Alternatively, mix 1 tablespoon of icing sugar with a drop of water to make a 'glue' and use instead. Stick the cake pearls onto the top of the cake, around the leaves. Leave to dry for a minimum of 2 hours before storing in an airtight container.

Wind a ribbon around the base of the cake, cut to fit and secure with pins or more cake glue. Serve!

AROMATIC CITRUS POLENTA CAKE

Beautifully moist and fragrant with star anise, cinnamon and cardamom, this cake is incredibly easy to make. Serve it on its own or with thick, velvety Greek yoghurt and a scattering of pomegranate seeds.

Serves: 8

Prep: 25 minutes, plus soaking time
Cook: 50 minutes, plus cooling time

For the cake:

40 g polenta
110 g ground almonds
200 g golden caster sugar
1½ level teaspoons baking powder
200 ml vegetable oil, plus extra
  for greasing
4 eggs, beaten
grated zest of 1 orange
grated zest of 1 unwaxed lemon
grated zest of 1 lime

For the syrup:

75 g Lyle's Golden Syrup
juice of 1 orange
juice of 1 lemon
juice of 1 lime
5 star anise
2 small cinnamon sticks
8 cardamom pods, lightly crushed

To serve:

200 g natural Greek yoghurt
110 g pomegranate seeds
2 teaspoons orange flower water

Oil a 20 x 6 cm non-stick cake tin and line the base with baking parchment (cut a second piece of parchment the same size as the one you use to line the base of the tin, for using later).

Place the polenta, ground almonds, caster sugar and baking powder in a mixing bowl and stir to combine. Mix the oil and eggs together in a bowl or jug, then stir into the polenta mixture with a wooden spoon to make a thick batter. Stir in the orange, lemon and lime zest.

Pour the batter into the prepared cake tin and place on the middle shelf of a cold oven, then set the temperature to 190°C/170°C fan/Gas Mark 5. Bake for 20 minutes, then crumple up the spare sheet of baking parchment, run it under cold water, shake to remove any excess water and place it over the tin to prevent the cake from over-browning. Bake for a further 30 minutes until rich brown in colour and a fine skewer inserted into the middle of the cake comes out clean.

Meanwhile, make the syrup by combining the golden syrup, citrus juices and all the spices in a small saucepan. Place over a low heat for 6–8 minutes, bring to the boil, then reduce the heat and simmer for 2 minutes until syrupy. Remove from the heat and set aside to allow the spices to infuse, then strain and reserve the spices.

Remove the cake from the oven, let it cool for 10 minutes in the tin, then turn it out onto a serving plate, carefully peeling off the baking parchment. Pierce the top of the cake all over with a fine skewer and, while it's still warm, spoon over the syrup. Set the soaked cake aside for 1–2 hours for it absorb the syrup.

Arrange all the spices from the syrup on top of the cake to decorate, and serve with bowls of Greek yoghurt and pomegranate seeds sprinkled with orange flower water.

CHERRY AND ALMOND CAKE

A tea party favourite, cherry and almond cake is a winner every time. Use natural-coloured glacé cherries, if you can get hold of them. Rinsing the sticky juices off the cherries and dusting them with flour before adding them to the cake mix stops them sinking to the bottom while the cake cooks.

Serves: 8–10

Prep: 20 minutes
Cook: 1 hour

200 g glacé cherries, rinsed and dried
    if sticky, then halved
75 g plain flour
175 g unsalted butter, plus extra
    for greasing
75 g Lyle's Golden Syrup
75 g caster sugar
3 eggs, at room temperature,
    lightly beaten
½ teaspoon almond extract
150 g self-raising flour
½ teaspoon baking powder
50 g ground almonds
40 g demerara sugar

Preheat the oven to 180°C/160°C fan/Gas Mark 4. Grease an 18 cm deep round cake tin with butter and line the base and sides with greaseproof paper.

Put 50 g of the halved glacé cherries to one side and toss the remainder with a little of the plain flour.

Place the butter, golden syrup and sugar in a bowl and beat by hand or with an electric hand mixer until light and creamy. Add the eggs a little at a time, beating well after each addition. It doesn't matter if the mixture curdles as it will come together once you add the flour. Add the almond extract. Sift together the plain and self-raising flours and baking powder into a bowl then beat into the butter and sugar mixture with the ground almonds until thoroughly mixed.

Stir the flour-dusted cherries into the cake mixture then spoon into the prepared tin and level the surface. Toss the reserved cherries with the demerara sugar and scatter them over the top of the cake, adding any remaining sugar. Bake for 1 hour, until well risen – a fine skewer inserted into the middle of the cake should come out clean. Remove from the oven and leave to cool for 10 minutes in the tin on a wire rack before turning out of the tin to cool completely (remove the greaseproof paper).

TANGY LEMON CHEESECAKE

Soft and creamy on top, with a crisp biscuit base, this luscious, tangy lemon cheesecake gives you the best of both worlds – and it doesn't take a lot of cooking. Best made and served the same day.

Serves: 8

Prep: 30 minutes
Cook: 2 minutes, plus chilling time

For the base:

175 g digestive biscuits
95 g unsalted butter, plus extra
    for greasing
1 tablespoon Lyle's Golden Syrup

For the lemon cream:

740 g mascarpone cheese
100 ml lemon juice (from 2½–3
    lemons)
grated zest of 2 lemons, plus extra
    to decorate
40 g Lyle's Golden Syrup, plus extra
    to drizzle
40 g golden caster sugar

To decorate:

225 g blueberries and blackberries (or
    seasonal berries of your choice)
Lyle's Golden Syrup, to drizzle

Lightly grease a 22 x 3.5 cm deep loose-bottomed tart or cake tin with butter. Break the biscuits into large pieces, then whizz them in the bowl of a food processor or crush them in a plastic bag with a rolling pin until you have fine crumbs. Pour the biscuit crumbs into a bowl.

Pop the butter and the golden syrup for the base in a small saucepan and heat gently until the butter has melted, then pour the mixture over the biscuit crumbs and stir until combined. Spoon into the prepared tin and press out to make a level base. Transfer to the fridge while you make the topping.

To make the lemon cream, mix the mascarpone, lemon juice and zest, golden syrup and sugar together in a bowl until smooth. Carefully spoon the mixture over the chilled biscuit base, smoothing the surface. Return to the fridge and chill until firm.

Remove the cheesecake from the fridge about 15 minutes before serving, so the biscuit base can soften a little. Carefully lift the cheesecake out of its tin then use a flat-bladed knife to remove it from the base and transfer it to a serving plate.

Get creative: arrange the fruits decoratively on top, drizzle over some golden syrup, scatter with lemon zest and serve. Lovely.

PARKIN

This old-fashioned spiced cake is perfect for making ahead – it becomes stickier and softer the longer you keep it, and can be stored in an airtight container for up to 2 weeks. Keeping the baking parchment on the cake once baked helps keep it moist.

Makes: 14 pieces

Prep: 20 minutes

Cook: 1–1¼ hours

225 g plain flour

¼ teaspoon salt

2 teaspoons ground allspice

2 teaspoons ground ginger

1 teaspoon bicarbonate of soda

225 g medium oatmeal

175 g golden syrup

150 g unsalted butter, plus extra
   for greasing

115 g soft light brown sugar

150 ml whole milk

1 large egg, beaten

Preheat the oven to 180°C/160°C fan/Gas Mark 4. Grease an 18 cm square cake tin with butter and line with baking parchment.

Sift the flour, salt, allspice, ginger and bicarbonate of soda into a bowl. Add the oatmeal and mix to combine. Make a well in the centre.

Place the golden syrup, butter, soft light brown sugar and milk in a saucepan and stir over a low heat until the sugar has dissolved. Pour into the dry mixture and add the egg then stir briskly until well blended.

Spoon the mixture into the prepared tin and bake for 1–1¼ hours until cooked through. A fine skewer inserted into the middle of the cake should come out clean. Leave the cake to cool for 10 minutes in the tin, then turn out onto a wire rack to cool.

Store in an airtight container, without removing the baking parchment, and leave for at least 1 week before cutting into 14 pieces and serving.

ZESTY ORANGE AND POPPY SEED CAKE

This orange and poppy seed cake, a lovely light mixture of sweet sponge and tangy citrus, looks impressive, but is simple to make.

Serves: 12

Prep: 1 hour
Cook: 45–50 minutes,
    plus cooling time

For the cake:

unsalted butter, for greasing
2 oranges
3 large eggs, at room temperature
250 g soft light brown sugar
295 g ground almonds
1 rounded teaspoon baking powder
1 rounded tablespoon poppy seeds

For the syrup:

4 small seedless satsumas or
    tangerines
juice of 1 orange
150 g Lyle's Golden Syrup, plus extra
    for drizzling

Grease a 23 cm loose-bottomed round springform cake tin with butter and line the base with greaseproof paper.

Place the oranges in a saucepan of cold water, bring to the boil then simmer for 30 minutes, or until they are tender when poked with a fine skewer. Transfer to a bowl of cold water to stop the cooking process and leave for 5 minutes. Once they're cool enough to handle, cut them into chunks and discard any pips. Blitz the oranges – peel and all – in the bowl of a food processor to make a smooth-ish pulp. Preheat the oven to 180°C/160°C fan/ Gas Mark 4.

Place the eggs and sugar in the bowl of a stand mixer and beat for 4–5 minutes until light and fluffy (alternatively, beat with an electric hand mixer in a bowl). Gently fold in one-third of the ground almonds then add the rest, followed by the baking powder, poppy seeds and orange pulp.

Pour the mixture into the prepared cake tin, smooth the top and bake for 45–50 minutes, until golden and a fine skewer inserted into the middle of the cake comes out clean. Remove from the oven, leave to cool in the tin for 10 minutes, then turn out onto a wire rack to cool completely. Discard the greaseproof paper.

To make the syrup, cut the satsumas or tangerines into 8–9 thin slices, skin and all (discarding the ends), and add them to a saucepan with the orange juice and golden syrup. Bring to the boil then simmer for 12–15 minutes, or until the skin of the satsumas or tangerines is tender and the syrup has reduced down and thickened a little. Carefully pour the syrup into a heat-proof bowl to cool.

Prick the cake all over with a fine skewer then spoon over the cooled syrup. Arrange the sliced satsumas or tangerines overlapping on top, lift the cake onto a serving plate, drizzle with extra golden syrup and serve.

LUXURY PANFORTE

Typically served with coffee or a glass of dessert wine at the end of a meal, this Italian spiced fruit and nut cake is sticky, chewy and utterly irresistible. It lasts for weeks stored in an airtight container.

Makes: 24 small wedges

Prep: 25 minutes
Cook: 40–45 minutes

1 sheet edible rice paper
110 g blanched almonds
110 g blanched hazelnuts
110 g unsalted shelled pistachios
150 g soft dried figs, quartered
75 g mixed candied peel
50 g dried cranberries
50 g plain flour
10 g cocoa powder
1 rounded teaspoon ground cinnamon
½ rounded teaspoon mixed spice
150 g Lyle's Golden Syrup
150 g golden caster sugar
25 g unsalted butter, plus extra
   for greasing
icing sugar, to dust (optional)

Preheat the oven to 170°C/150°C fan/Gas Mark 3. Grease a 20 cm sandwich tin with butter and line the base with a disc of edible rice paper, cut to size.

Combine the blanched almonds and hazelnuts, pistachios, figs, candied peel and cranberries in a large bowl.

Sift the flour, cocoa powder, ground cinnamon and mixed spice into a separate bowl then stir it into the fruit and nut mixture.

Place the golden syrup, sugar and butter in a small non-stick saucepan over a low heat and stir with a wooden spoon for about 5 minutes until very hot and the sugar has dissolved. Tip the hot mixture into the bowl of dry ingredients. Stir well and spoon into the prepared tin, pressing the mixture down firmly to make sure the surface is level.

Bake for 40–45 minutes until the panforte is a deep brown colour and bubbling a little at the edges. Remove from the oven, leave to cool slightly, then turn out onto a wire rack to cool completely. Lightly dust with icing sugar, if using, and cut into 24 small wedges to serve.

ELEGANT GOLDEN SCONES

A beautifully light, soft take on traditional scones – the magic of golden syrup makes these delights an afternoon tea dream. They're extra special served just slightly warm from the oven.

Makes: 8 scones

Prep: 15 minutes
Cook: 15–18 minutes

30 g Lyle's Golden Syrup, plus
   1 tablespoon for brushing
295 g self-raising flour, plus extra
   for dusting and dipping
30 g golden caster sugar
120 ml whole milk
120 ml single cream
jam or more Lyle's Golden Syrup,
   and clotted or whipped cream,
   to serve

Preheat the oven to 180°C/160°C fan/Gas Mark 4 and line a baking tray with silicone or baking parchment. Gently warm the golden syrup in a small pan, just until it loosens (do not boil).

Combine the flour and sugar in a bowl. Make a well in the centre, then pour in the warm golden syrup, milk and cream. Quickly and lightly mix until just combined. (The mixture will be deliciously sticky.)

Turn the mixture out onto a floured surface and gently pat the dough into a rectangular shape (no need to roll it) with the well-floured palms of your hands. You are looking for the dough to be about 2 cm thick. The less you handle the dough the lighter the scones will be.

Dip a 6 cm plain round cutter into a small bowl of flour before stamping out the scones. Press the cutter down into the dough without twisting, or the scones will rise unevenly. Place the scones, set apart, on the prepared baking tray. Lightly re-form any trimmings to make more scones.

Bake on the middle shelf for 15–18 minutes, until well risen and golden. Remove from the oven and leave to cool on a wire rack. Heat 1 tablespoon of golden syrup in a small saucepan and use it to brush the tops of the scones. When cool, split and serve with cream and jam or golden syrup.

picture overleaf »

SWEET BITES

TOFFEE RICE BARS

So simple to make, yet so moreish. What's not to love?

Makes: 25 bars

Prep: 10 minutes

115 g unsalted butter, plus extra
    for greasing
75 g caster sugar
75 g soft dark brown sugar
3 level tablespoons Lyle's
    Golden Syrup
397 g can condensed milk
115 g Rice Krispies
100 g dried fruit, such as cranberries
    or sour cherries

Grease a 20 cm shallow square cake tin with butter and line it with baking parchment.

Place the butter and both sugars in a large non-stick saucepan and melt together over a low heat, then add the golden syrup and condensed milk and slowly bring to the boil while stirring continuously. Simmer for 1 minute, then remove from the heat.

Add the Rice Krispies and dried fruit, fold together, then transfer the mixture into the prepared tin. Leave to cool, then cut into bars or small squares.

Lyle's Tip

If you're making these with children, give them some coloured sugar sprinkles or edible silver or gold dust to scatter into the mix before you pour it into the tin to set.

BOUQUET CAKE POPS

You could cheat and use shop-bought sponge for these cake pops, but it's fun to make them from scratch if you have the time. You will need 30 lollipop sticks and a block of polystyrene pierced to hold the cake pops.

Makes: 30 cake pops

Prep: 1½ hours, plus chilling time
Cook: 25–30 minutes,
    plus cooling time

For the cake:

125 g unsalted butter, softened,
    plus extra for greasing
2 tablespoons Lyle's Golden Syrup
95 g golden caster sugar
2 eggs, beaten
125 g self-raising flour
grated zest of 1 small orange
1 tablespoon orange juice
1 tablespoon whole milk

For the cake balls:

75 g full-fat cream cheese
2 tablespoons Lyle's Golden Syrup
110 g icing sugar, plus extra for
    dusting

For coating and decorating:

200 g white chocolate, broken
    into pieces
decorative sugar flowers
icing sugar, to dust

Preheat the oven to 160°C/140°C fan/Gas Mark 3. Grease a 20 cm loose-bottomed round cake tin and line it with baking parchment.

Combine the butter, golden syrup and caster sugar in a bowl and beat together until soft and creamy. Add the eggs a little at a time and beat until well incorporated. Sift over the flour and fold it in with a metal spoon. Stir in the orange zest, juice and milk.

Spoon the mixture into the prepared cake tin and bake in the oven for 25–30 minutes until well risen and golden brown. A fine skewer inserted into the middle of the cake should come out clean.

Remove from the oven and leave the cake to cool in the tin for 10 minutes then turn it out onto a wire rack to cool completely. Discard the paper, then blitz the cake in a food processor to make a crumb-like consistency and tip the crumbled cake into a bowl.

Add the cream cheese, golden syrup and icing sugar to the processor and quickly process until smooth. Stir into the cake crumbs and combine to make a moist mixture. Roll into 30 equal-sized balls, place on a tray, cover and chill for 1 hour or until firm.

To coat the balls, melt the chocolate in the microwave, stirring every 20 seconds, or place the bowl over a pan of simmering water and stir until melted. Remove the cake balls from the fridge. Dip one end of the lollipop sticks (about 1 cm) into the chocolate, then push the sticks halfway through the centres of the firm cake balls. Dip the cake pops one at a time into the chocolate, ensuring that they are covered right up to the top of the sticks to secure. Gently tap them against the side of the bowl to remove any excess, then decorate with sugar flowers while they are still wet. Stand upright in the polystyrene block for about 30 minutes until firm. Store at room temperature for 2 days, or chill for up to 1 week, covered with parchment so they don't sweat. Lightly dust with icing sugar and serve in glasses.

SWEET FILO CHEESE PASTRIES

These crispy, golden pastries with a sweet dip are dangerously moreish, and perfect served with coffee at the end of a meal. Sprinkle the pastry with sesame seeds if you like, before baking.

Makes: 16 pastries

Prep: 5 minutes

Cook: 10 minutes

250 g mascarpone cheese

2 tablespoons sultanas

grated zest and juice of
   1 lemon

1 tablespoon Lyle's Golden Syrup

4 sheets filo pastry

30 g butter, melted

For the dipping sauce:

2 tablespoons Lyle's Golden Syrup

juice of 1 lemon

Preheat the oven to 200°C/180°C fan/Gas Mark 6 and line a baking sheet with baking parchment.

Mix the mascarpone with the sultanas, lemon zest and juice and golden syrup in a bowl.

Cut each sheet of filo pastry into 4 equal lengths, and use a pastry brush to brush them with melted butter.

Put a generous teaspoon of the mascarpone filling onto a filo pastry strip, at the end nearest you, then fold one of the bottom corners up over the filling to meet the opposite edge of the pastry, making a triangle shape. Keep folding, with the filling enclosed, until you reach the top of the pastry strip. Brush with more butter to give them extra crispness, and repeat with the remaining strips and filling.

Transfer to the lined baking sheet and bake in the oven for 10 minutes.

Meanwhile, whisk the syrup with the lemon juice to make the dipping sauce. Serve the pastries warm with the dipping sauce.

CHOCOLATE TRUFFLES

Easy as anything to make, these melt-in-the-mouth syrupy truffles make a lovely gift when packed into a pretty box. A melon baller is a useful tool here, if you happen to have one lurking in your cutlery drawer. These truffles keep well, chilled, in an airtight container for up to 4 days.

Makes: 30 truffles

Prep: 30 minutes
Cook: 4–5 minutes, plus setting time

250 g dark chocolate (70 per cent cocoa solids), broken into pieces
120 ml double cream
40 g unsalted butter, cubed
2 tablespoons Lyle's Golden Syrup
1 level tablespoon icing sugar
1 level tablespoon cocoa powder
20 g toasted, chopped hazelnuts

Set a heat-proof bowl over a small saucepan of boiling water, making sure the bottom of the bowl doesn't touch the water. Add the chocolate, cream, butter and golden syrup and stir occasionally for 4–5 minutes, or until the chocolate and butter have melted, and the mixture is well combined and glossy. Remove from the heat, transfer to another bowl and leave to cool and set for 3–4 hours.

Line a baking tray with greaseproof paper. Dip a melon baller or teaspoon into a bowl of hot water then scoop the chocolate truffle mixture into 30 balls, dipping the baller in the hot water after making each ball (if using a teaspoon, roll the mixture in balls with your hands). Place the truffles on the lined tray. Place the icing sugar, cocoa powder and pistachios in 3 separate small bowls. Roll 10 of the truffles in each of the different mixtures to coat evenly. Firm up in the fridge for 1 hour before serving or packing into gift box(es).

Lyle's Tip

Use good quality milk or white chocolate in place of the dark chocolate, if you prefer lighter truffles.

PEANUT BRITTLE

Salty, sweet and crunchy, with the warmth of golden syrup running through it, this is a cracking little treat. Wrap or bag up as a gift, or crumble it over your favourite ice cream.

Makes: plenty!

Prep: 5 minutes, plus setting time
Cook: 25 minutes

60 g unsalted butter, plus extra for greasing
180 g caster sugar
200 g Lyle's Golden Syrup
200 g salted peanuts

Lightly grease a baking tray.

Put the butter and sugar in a saucepan with 1 tablespoon of water and heat slowly over a gentle heat, stirring all the time, until the butter melts.

Add the golden syrup and continue to heat and stir until the sugar dissolves. Bring to a gentle boil and stir continuously for about 10 minutes, until it turns into an amber caramel. Test by dropping a tiny bit of the mixture into a bowl of ice-cold water. If it immediately hardens, you're ready to add the peanuts (if not, continue to boil and test again a minute or two later).

Add the peanuts and keep heating and stirring. The peanuts will have cooled the mixture down a little, so test another drop in a bowl of ice-cold water. If it hardens in the water, it's ready.

Carefully pour the hot mixture onto the greased baking tray and leave to harden for about 30 minutes.

Break into pieces with a toffee hammer or with the handle of a heavy knife.

Lyle's Tips

If you have a sugar thermometer, the temperature of the caramel should reach 154°C.

Try using roasted salted or unsalted almonds or hazelnuts in place of the peanuts.

CARAMEL POPCORN CLUSTERS

To give these pleasing sweet treats a richer, grown-up edge, with a hint of bitterness, swap the golden syrup for black treacle. You can make the popcorn clusters up to a week in advance, and store them in an airtight container.

Makes: about 24 clusters

Prep: 10 minutes
Cook: 25 minutes, plus setting time

100 g bag microwave sweet popcorn
185 g unsalted butter
110 g Lyle's Golden Syrup
275 g soft light brown sugar

Line 2 baking trays with baking parchment.

Microwave the popcorn according to the packet instructions, discard any un-popped kernels, then pour it into a heat-proof bowl.

Combine the butter, golden syrup and sugar in a large heavy-based saucepan over a low heat, and stir constantly with a wooden spoon for about 10 minutes, until the sugar has dissolved.

Once the sugar has dissolved, bring to the boil without stirring (otherwise the sugar may crystallise) until the mixture reaches 149–154°C or the 'hard crack' stage on a sugar thermometer. It will take 10–12 minutes to reach this stage. If you don't have a thermometer you can check it is ready by dropping a teaspoon of the mixture into a bowl of ice-cold water. It should harden instantly and, when removed, be brittle and easy to break. If not, continue to boil the mixture, and check again after a few minutes.

Carefully pour the caramel over the popcorn and, using two large spoons, very quickly stir everything together before the caramel cools and sets. Spoon into clusters onto the baking trays and leave to cool and harden.

GOLDEN HONEYCOMB

Gorgeous golden honeycomb pieces – with bite. Cook up these chunks in a flash, then scatter over desserts for added crunch.

Serves: 10

Prep: 10 minutes

Cook: 10 minutes, plus setting time

unsalted butter, for greasing

4 tablespoons Lyle's Golden Syrup

200 g caster sugar

3 teaspoons bicarbonate of soda

Grease a 20 cm square cake tin with butter.

Place the golden syrup and sugar in a large saucepan, bring to the boil and then simmer over a low heat for 5–10 minutes until you have a golden caramel. Test the syrup by dropping a little into a bowl of ice-cold water. If it immediately hardens, it's ready.

Remove the pan from the heat and add the bicarbonate of soda. Beat it in quickly as the mixture will foam up instantly.

Carefully pour the bubbling mixture immediately into the greased cake tin. Leave to set at room temperature until hard and brittle, then break into bite-sized chunks.

Lyle's Tip

Crunch it up nice and small to add to ice cream, or leave it generously chunky to pick at when peckish. It makes a perfect gift, too.

JEWELLED CHOCOLATE DROPS

Simple and quick to make, these little fruited chocolate drops make a gorgeous gift packed in cellophane bags or teeny boxes. Alternatively, serve as an after-dinner treat. You can make them up to 5 days in advance and store them between sheets of parchment paper in a lidded container in the fridge.

Makes: 16 chocolate drops

Prep: 20 minutes
Cook: 5 minutes, plus setting time

110 g dark chocolate (minimum
    70 per cent cocoa solids), broken
    into pieces
2 teaspoons Lyle's Golden Syrup
50 g dried fruits, such as cranberries,
    blueberries, chopped mixed peel
    and goji berries
25 g flaked almonds and pistachios,
    roughly chopped
icing sugar, to dust
cocoa powder, to dust

Line 2 baking trays with baking parchment.

Half-fill a small saucepan with water and bring to the boil. Place the chocolate in a small heat-proof bowl, sit the bowl over the pan of water, remove from the heat and leave to melt. Alternatively, melt the chocolate in the microwave in 20-second bursts (to make sure it doesn't burn). Stir the golden syrup into the melted chocolate then set aside for about 10 minutes to cool and thicken a little.

Meanwhile, draw 16 x 5 cm circles on the parchment paper, spaced apart a little. Drop a teaspoon of the warm chocolate mixture onto the circles, using the back of the spoon to spread it out evenly.

Sprinkle a little of each of the fruit and nuts onto the chocolate, then transfer the trays to the fridge until the chocolate has set.

To serve, spoon a little icing sugar and cocoa powder into a small sieve and very lightly dust the chocolate drops.

NOT-JUST-FOR-KIDS
CHOCOLATE CRISPIES

Childishly simple to concoct, these are everyone's favourite – whether you make them yourself, or with a little one. Don't fancy Rice Krispies? The recipe works just as well with cornflakes or shredded cereal (especially if you're nesting mini Easter eggs on top). Like a more grown-up version? Just stir a couple of tablespoons of strong coffee into the melted chocolate mixture as you go.

Makes: 12 crispies

Prep: 15 minutes, plus chilling time
Cook: 5 minutes

110 g dark chocolate (minimum
    70 per cent cocoa solids),
    broken into chunks
50 g unsalted butter, cubed
50 g Lyle's Golden Syrup
75 g Rice Krispies or puffed
    brown rice

Line a 12-hole muffin tin with paper cases.

Pop the chocolate, butter and golden syrup into a heat-proof bowl and set it over a small saucepan of simmering water, making sure the bowl doesn't touch the water. Let it heat for about 5 minutes – stirring from time to time – until the chocolate and butter have melted and the mixture is smooth. Turn off the heat and remove the bowl from the pan, then gently stir in the Rice Krispies or puffed brown rice with a metal spoon until they are completely covered in chocolate.

Scoop the mixture into the paper cases then chill for about 1 hour, or until the chocolate has set. Store in an airtight container in the fridge until ready to eat (they keep for about 1 week).

POPCORN TOFFEE APPLES

You will need 8–10 wooden ice-lolly sticks, cake-pop sticks or twigs. If you have any spare toffee and popcorn after making the toffee apples, just stir them together in a bowl, quickly spoon into clusters on some baking parchment and leave to harden.

Makes: 8–10 toffee apples

Prep: 25 minutes
Cook: 25 minutes

8–10 small Cox's apples, stalks twisted off

100 g bag microwave sweet and salty popcorn

225 g Lyle's Golden Syrup

450 g demerara sugar

110 g unsalted butter

1 tablespoon red or white wine vinegar

Line 2 baking trays with baking parchment. Put the apples in a large heat-proof bowl, pour over just-boiled water to cover and then quickly and carefully pour it away. This will remove any wax coating from the apples and will help the toffee to stick. Rub the apples dry.

Push the twigs (make sure they are clean), lolly sticks or cake-pop sticks halfway into the core of the apples at the stalk end. Microwave the popcorn, according to the packet instructions, and transfer it to a bowl.

Combine the golden syrup, sugar, butter and vinegar in a large heavy-based saucepan and stir constantly over a low heat with a wooden spoon for about 15 minutes, until the sugar has dissolved. Bring to the boil without stirring (otherwise the sugar may crystallise), until the mixture reaches 149–154°C, or the 'hard-crack' stage on a sugar thermometer. If you don't have a thermometer you can check that the toffee is ready by dropping a teaspoon of the mixture into a bowl of ice-cold water. It should harden instantly and, when removed, be brittle and easy to break. If you can still squash the toffee, continue to boil it.

Remove the pan from the heat and, tilting it, quickly and carefully dip the apples one at a time into the toffee, holding them by the stick and twirling them, to completely cover. Let any excess toffee drip away before quickly scattering with popcorn while the toffee is still hot, then place on the lined baking trays to harden. (This is easier to do with help, with one person dipping and the other scattering with popcorn.) If you find the toffee becomes too thick because the temperature has dropped, just heat it up again.

Once set, store in an airtight container in a dry place (not the fridge) and eat within 24 hours or the toffee will soften.

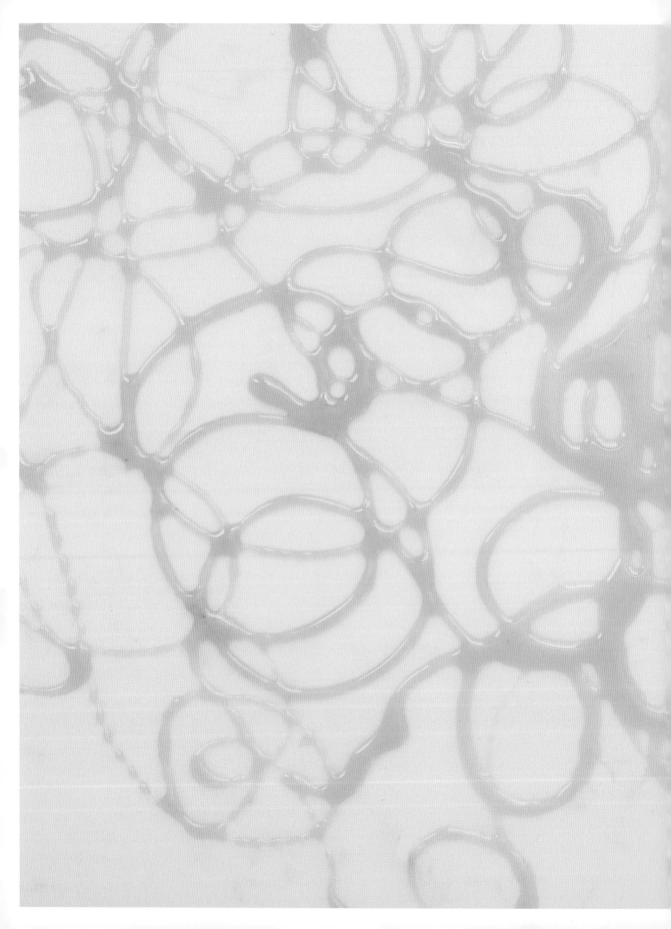

INDEX

Senior Commissioning Editor: Nicky Hill
Project manager and editor: Laura Nickoll
Designer and art director: Miranda Harvey
Photographer: Clare Winfield
Food stylist: Rosie Reynolds
Prop stylist: Tony Hutchinson
Production manager: Katherine Thornton
European Product & Licensing Manager, Tate & Lyle Sugars: Sara Harrison

Simon & Schuster would like to thank Karen Farrington for the introduction
and Debbie Major for additional recipe writing and testing.

Picture credit (p19): Simon Smith

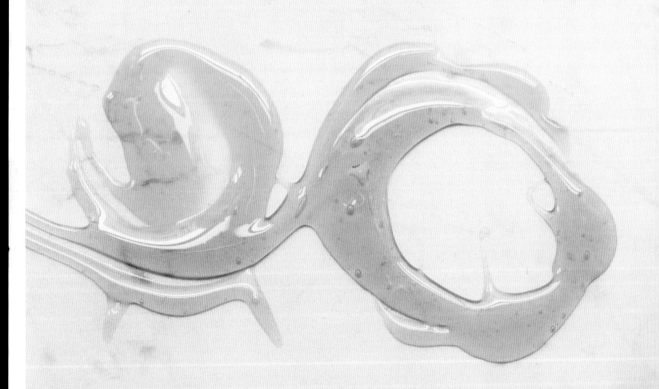